D1380463

THE BOOK OF RUTH

THE BOOK OF RUTH

So Naomi returned, and Ruth the Moabitess,
her daughter-in-law, with her, which returned
out of the country of Moab: and they came to
Bethlehem in the beginning of barley harvest

RUTH 1:22

JOHN METCALFE

THE PUBLISHING TRUST
Church Road, Tylers Green, Penn, Buckinghamshire.

Printed and Published by
John Metcalfe Publishing Trust
Church Road, Tylers Green
Penn, Buckinghamshire

—

—

First Published 1988

—

ISBN 1 870039 17 3

—

CONTENTS

THE BOOK OF RUTH

I

A Famine in the Land

BOOK OF RUTH 1:1, *There was a famine in the land.*

THE book of Ruth is set against the farming background of old testament Israel at the time of the judges, the narrative revolving around a series of agricultural events. It is impossible to understand the book without having some insight into the significance of these events, not only because of their being interwoven with the feasts into the religious life and worship of the people, but also because they appear in the scripture in a prophetic and typical light as signs of the coming blessings of the promised new testament. That is to say, every event of agricultural importance to this farming people had a spiritual significance of great depth, not only directly in that community, but also as figurative of a promised age yet to come.

1

For example, the feast of the passover took place when the first crop of the year, the barley, was green in the ear, and was just beginning to ripen. Passover was ushered in by the agricultural event of the ripening barley harvest. The slaying of the passover lamb was not only of great moment to every household in Israel, but what it typified was of even greater significance in the new testament: 'Christ our passover is sacrificed for us', I Cor. 5:7.

What of the ripening barley? What does that signify? On the morrow after the sabbath immediately following the passover, the first few early-ripe stalks of barley were cut to form a sheaf. This sheaf was lifted up to heaven and waved before the LORD in the tabernacle of the congregation. Now the morrow after the sabbath was the first day of the week, the third day after that on which Christ our passover was slain, the very day on which Christ rose from the dead.

From the morrow after the sabbath the Israelites were to count a week of weeks—forty-nine days—during which the whole harvest would be gathered, winnowed, and the corn brought into the garner. By the time the week of weeks had been counted the harvest was home, and the corn laid up. It was 'When the day of Pentecost was fully come', Acts 2:1, that the Holy Ghost came down and filled the company of the disciples, so forming the church, the body of Christ.

How great therefore is the prophetic significance of the sequence of agricultural events woven into the worship of Israel around which the book of Ruth revolves, and how important it is to the right understanding of the narrative that this should be opened and discerned. Although the events took place thousands of years ago, their spiritual impact is not to be limited to the Israelites of that time. The spiritual importance of these things could hardly be more contemporary or more relevant to our own times.

The book of Ruth opens with the words 'Now it came to pass in the days when the judges ruled, that there was a famine in the land', Ruth 1:1. But had the judges ruled rightly, there would never have been a famine in the land: What kind of an agricultural event is a famine? It is a disaster. Nevertheless Moses had taught them 'If thou shalt hearken diligently unto the voice of the LORD thy God, to observe and to do all his commandments which I command thee this day, that the LORD thy God will set thee on high above all nations of the earth', Deut. 28:1. So that 'Blessed shalt thou be in the field; blessed shall be the fruit of thy ground'; and 'blessed shall be thy basket and thy store.' Then what was this 'famine in the land' when the judges ruled? It was 'But if thou wilt not hearken unto the voice of the LORD thy God, to observe to do all his commandments and his statutes which I command thee this day; that all these curses shall come upon thee, and overtake thee', Deut. 28:18. 'Cursed shalt thou be in the field; cursed shall be thy basket and thy store; cursed shall be the fruit of thy land'; and 'because of the wickedness of thy doings, whereby thou hast forsaken me, the LORD shall make the pestilence cleave unto thee, until he have consumed thee from off the land.'

In the days when the judges ruled 'there was a famine in the land'. Then what kind of rule was this? The judges were not ruling for the LORD, else there would have been blessing. But there was famine: there was cursing. Then over what did they rule? They ruled over disobedience, and answered not a word. This condition is described in the last chapter and verse of the previous book, the book of Judges, 'In those days there was no king in Israel: every man did that which was right in his own eyes.' As to that, it is described in Judges 17:1-5: Theft, lawlessness, disobedience, idolatry, presumption, and all in the name of religion. Why? Because, Judges 17:6, 'In those days there was no king in Israel, but every man did that which was right in his own eyes.' And this was the rule of the judges? 'And there was a famine in the land.'

Every man did that which was right in his own eyes? In the name of the LORD, no doubt? With a mouthful of scriptures, surely? But Moses commanded, when they came into the land from Egypt through that howling wilderness, 'Ye shall not do after all the doings that we do here this day, every man whatsoever is right in his own eyes', Deut. 12:8. On the contrary, 'Thou shalt hearken to the voice of the LORD thy God, to keep all his commandments which I command thee this day, to do that which is right in the eyes of the LORD thy God', Deut. 13:18. Then the judges who ruled ignored what was right in the eyes of the LORD, and condoned what was right every man in his own eyes, prudently holding their peace to obtain the favour of the people. But 'there was a famine in the land.'

Next we read that 'A certain man of Bethlehem-judah went to sojourn in the country of Moab, he, and his wife, and his two sons', Ruth 1:1. The name of this man was Elimelech, which signifies 'God is king'. But to Elimelech God was not king. Elimelech did that which was right in his own eyes, he went to Moab. But this was evil in the eyes of the LORD, and it was an evil into which the man led his household with him. Why was it evil? Because 'An Ammonite or Moabite shall not enter into the congregation of the LORD; even to their tenth generation shall they not enter into the congregation of the LORD for ever', Deut. 23:3. And shall Israel go down to Moab for bread?

But Elimelech—disdaining to search out the cause of the famine—despised repentance. He forsook Bethlehem, which means 'House of bread', and, turning from the LORD's inheritance, sought for bread in the heathen land of Moab. Afterwards he found Moabitish wives for his sons, despite that Moses had commanded 'Thou shalt make no covenant with them, nor show mercy unto them: neither shalt thou make marriages with them; thy daughter thou shalt not give unto his son, nor his daughter shalt thou take unto thy son', Deut. 7:2,3.

This was an abomination in Israel, to cause the heart of Moab to rejoice at the fall of the people of the LORD. 'We have heard of the pride of Moab; he is very proud: even of his haughtiness, and his pride, and his wrath: but his lies shall not be so', Isa. 16:6.

Elimelech went to the heathen for bread because there was none in Israel. But why was there none in Israel? And why was there bread in Moab? Because Moab's judgment awaits him without remedy at the last day, whereas Israel is chastened of the LORD to bring him to repentance. 'He showeth his word unto Jacob, his statutes and his judgments unto Israel. He hath not dealt so with any nation: and as for his judgments, they have not known them. Praise ye the LORD', Psalm 147:19,20. But Elimelech thought to escape the consequences of Israel's sin, going down to Moab, a nation in which God's judgments were not known. And shall he escape?

Elimelech should have fallen upon his face in Bethlehemjudah, confessing to God, and saying 'I have sinned and thy people, and done this evil in thy sight', submitting to the chastening of the LORD under the famine. But because now no chastening for the present seemeth to be pleasant, but grievous, rather than submit to this chastening, Elimelech's house left God's land of famine, where God would deal with them, and went down to the fields of Moab for bread.

This came to pass in the days when the judges ruled. Indeed, all this folly on the part of a comparatively obscure man in a relatively little known town stemmed from the toleration of evil in the land under the rule of the judges. 'The wicked walk on every side, when the vilest men are exalted', Psalm 12:8. This brought down the famine. Under such chastening conditions, God's judgments should have been owned and admitted, the people should have sought the LORD, they should have repented from the heart, and the wicked should have been turned out of their places, the vilest men being overthrown.

That the judges ruled by shifting expediency, and not by the righteousness of God is evident, for 'there was a famine in the land'. That the corruption of the leaders encouraged the people in worldliness and sin is equally clear, because 'a certain man of Bethlehem-judah went to sojourn in the country of Moab.' Why? Because there was bread in Moab. Among the heathen. The equivalent, in new testament terms, is called 'the world'. What have the apostles to say, then, of the people of God seeking the methods, appearances, and benefits of worldly fruitfulness, in order to disguise their barrenness of the power of God, and cover over the truth that the judgments of God lie heavy upon them?

The apostles have this to say: 'Ye adulterers and adulteresses, know ye not that the friendship of the world is enmity with God? whosoever therefore will be a friend of the world is the enemy of God', Jas. 4:4. Mark that, the enemy of God. 'Love not the world, neither the things that are in the world. If any man love the world, the love of the Father is not in him', I John 2:15. These things being so, the people of God may say in every age and generation, 'We know that we are of God, and the whole world lieth in wickedness', I John 5:19. Then what is this going down to Moab for bread, this conformity with the world in order to appear fruitful? What has happened to the religion of our fathers? Where is the power of God? There is a famine of the power of God.

Our leaders are like the judges, whom the prophet calls 'blind watchmen: they are all ignorant, they are all dumb dogs, they cannot bark; sleeping, lying down, loving to slumber. Yea, they are greedy dogs which can never have enough, and they are shepherds that cannot understand: they all look to their own way, every one for his gain, from his quarter', Isa. 56:10,11. Such watchmen as these will say, 'We are leading you all right: there is nothing wrong. We are leading you according to good judgment and sound wisdom.' Then why is there a famine? 'For the Lord hath called for a famine',

A Famine in the Land

II Kings 8:1. What famine? 'Behold, the days come, saith the Lord GOD, that I will send a famine in the land, not a famine of bread, nor a thirst for water, but of hearing the words of the LORD', Amos 8:11.

That is what we have today, there is a parallel, spiritually: it is the same condition as in the days when the judges ruled. Why is it so long since we have known a true revival of religion? Where is the awesome sense of the majesty, the power and the fear of God, the mighty power of the Holy Ghost sweeping over the congregation, the breaking in from another realm, from eternity, of the unearthly light of the irresistible word of God? Why is it so many years—yea, generations—since there came forth from heaven the dew, the freshness, the glory of the doctrine and truth of the most high God? Why are men so afraid to reprove and rebuke the real sins of the age that grieve the Holy Spirit of God? Why are they such flatterers of each other? 'Oh, but we have to move with the times', they say, 'We must keep up with modern trends.' Their language is 'There is nothing for it, nothing else we can do, we must go with the current movements.' So we get this kind of judging, Eli's judging, a judging worse than that of the days when the judges ruled in the book of Ruth.

But God has withdrawn. There is a famine. And as Elimelech went to Moab for bread, so these have gone to the world to make up for the famine of the word and power of God. But when God has withdrawn, when there is the hiding of his face, the people ought to fall upon their faces, the priests should howl all night, the king and the rulers, the princes, should rend their hearts with their garments, putting on sackcloth and ashes, and repent themselves of all their wickedness against the LORD. Oh, says someone, but that is all old testament. But I can tell you this: many a godly minister, many of the saints in times past in the church of God, have put on sackcloth, weeping night after night, crying with bitter lamentation, fasting day after day, for the

7

calamities that had come and were coming upon the church of God. And God was entreated of them, and the power fell upon the people, there were days of heaven upon earth.

Is that what we find today? Do you see this in your generation? Can you find such people? Is it the heart-broken cry of a people for their God, thirsting for God, for the living God, that we hear? Is it Rachel weeping for her children? No. No, it is the sound of feet marching down to Moab, going to the world for another kind of bread than that which obtains in God's inheritance. Far from crying 'Oh that thou wouldest rend the heavens, that thou wouldest come down', far from a broken and a contrite heart, there is every invention that the ingenuity of man can devise, to pretend that all is well.

Every kind of imitation of the world may be found in the professing church, every adaption of theatre and entertainment, a constantly changing round of turns and activities, in case the people become bored. This is nowhere more true than in what passes for evangelism. And now, the people having since become infatuated with the charismatic delusion, the unthinkable has happened: in a moment they have thrown down centuries of building up, going back to the antichrist, the man of sin, the system of Babylon, popery, all of a sudden dismantling the massive bulwarks of the Reformation with reckless abandon. This is the bread to which they are going, because, to them, the old ways do not work any more. Things have changed, you see. God has changed, and we have changed, and the churches have changed. The Bible has changed, the world has changed, and, their judges tell them, they need to be geared to the times. And if there is no bread in the old, boring inheritance of their fathers, what matters, if there is bread and to spare in the exciting new ecumenical fields of Rome?

There is a famine in the land, however. And, alas, the judges cannot rule, and the people love to have it so. But God judges, and rules over all. We have this state of affairs in evangelicalism particularly, where we are being led by corrupt and flattering judges of specious appearance. They will cry out 'Do not judge'. But in order to occupy their place they themselves set an example in evangelicalism, and by this they judge. And what kind of judgment is it? It is no judgment at all, not of themselves, nor for God, neither yet for the good of the people. What judgment, when Anglicans, with their 'evangelical' train, have gone a whoring after popery, followed by the so-called free churches, as the prophecy of John is fulfilled in them, 'all the world wondered after the beast', Rev. 13:3?

Vast spiritual movements have taken place, immense unseen powers have been deployed, everything leading up to the end. The people have been carried along by successive waves of mass evangelism, borne on succeeding charismatic tides, modernists and evangelicals have merged, the Bible has disintegrated into a multitude of optional versions, as, progressively, men have forsaken the old paths and removed the old landmarks. To this, we are told, we must consent. We are not to judge. It is a corruption of judgment which we are expected to accept. Largely the rule of these judges has prevailed. But there is still a people upon whom they cannot foist their counterfeit bread, any more than their corrupt judgment. Such a people has an invincible argument against the depravity of the judges: they are starving. For all the Moabitish bread, there remains a hungry people of God groaning in the land. They are not many. I do not believe there are many people of God. I believe there are very few people of God, and this is in itself a dreadful witness of God's judgments.

In contrast with such an elect people, there is a vast body, a multitude, who profess to be Christians, and who are content enough that 'the judges rule'. To these people there exists no famine. They are not hungry. With them there is no hungering and thirsting after righteousness. No mourning. No weeping.

No aching. No affliction. No, following their judges, they have taken Jesus as their saviour, as they say, and now brightly commend the same process to others. There is no interior conviction of sin, no sensation of being shut up to the wrath of God, no sounding of the curse of the law in their ears, no awareness of blackness, darkness, tempest, or the voice of words, no experience of the breaking forth within them of the great deep of inbred corruption and depravity. Consequently there is no soul-melting, heart-broken view of the redeemer vicariously in the place of sin and death under the judgment of Almighty God, no spiritual revelation or application of the blood of Christ, no interior enlightenment by the rays of divine glory streaming from the face of the Son of God. No doctrine, no truth, no experience, no justification. No cross, and no offence. Not a strait gate or a narrow way in sight.

But the Holy Ghost teaches, and holy scripture records, that it is God himself—Father, Son, and Holy Ghost—who by his mighty power justifies freely by grace. 'When it pleased God', says the apostle Paul, 'When it pleased God to reveal his Son in me.' That is not Paul's taking Jesus, or 'claiming' salvation. But by grace from God, out of heaven, by the revelation of the mystery, by the power of the Holy Ghost, Paul was saved: 'not of works, lest any man should boast.' Salvation is of the LORD. Many, who halt between two opinions, will say 'There is something in that'. But they will carry on in their set ways, neither hungering nor thirsting, apathetic under their old judges. These are the foolish virgins.

There is a famine, a famine of the hearing of the words of God; and a thirsting, a thirsting for the work of the Holy Ghost in salvation. And there are mourners in Zion who weep for such a divine work, day and night they weep, they cry for bread from heaven, they weep for the living fountains of waters. Yes, and there are watchmen still upon the walls of spiritual Jerusalem which shall never hold their peace, day nor night: they make mention of the LORD, they keep not silence, they give him no rest till he establish, till he make Jerusalem a praise in the earth.

This is in stark contrast with the arrangement and organisation of man, in which men and women making a decision, as they call it, is the object. Where was that on the Damascus road? For nearly two hundred years we have had a series of strong, forceful, charismatic personalities from America, employing the methods of mass persuasion to promote decisions from the vast numbers in their highly organised rallies and crusades. This entire system is geared to the closing minutes of the address. The singing, the solos, the supporting cast, the use of theatre and the methods of the hustings, all come down to the emotion charged tones of the 'Evangelist', as he is called, against the soft background of the crooning choir, to produce the 'results' for which the personality was hired for reward in the beginning.

There is nothing, absolutely nothing, of this in the scriptures. This does not even remotely resemble the evangelism of the new testament. In the new testament, under the apostles, the evangel was full of doctrinal content, it was preached, not 'offered', and God did the work not man. In the scriptures the evangelist was not paid, the singular work of the Holy Ghost brought in the church, and there was one church, gathered and united under the preaching of the gospel. With these latter-day counterfeits, it is 'the church of your choice', a lawless, unevangelical endorsement of divided sectarianism, by a 'gospel' so watered-down that far from bringing in the church, it could not—and must not—possibly offend any of the participating sects, especially the Anglican and papist sects. This system is man's system, in which to their shame many real children of God have been seduced for advantage, a system which has steadily and irrevocably deteriorated, merging with the emotionally charged charismatic dissolution at the last, ending with the union of papist and Protestant, Romanist and evangelical, without an evangel, without evangelism, and without an evangelist in the new testament sense. This is that delusion which God sends in the last days upon the disobedient, whereunto they were appointed.

Therefore we see not our signs: there is no more any prophet; Ps. 74:9. We see people professing 'Jesus', as they call him, whilst remaining carnal, worldly, and trifling with the pleasures of this present age. We see a famine of the work of God. The work of God slays what is carnal, and brings in what is spiritual; it takes worldliness out of the heart, and fills the soul with heavenly glory; it crucifies one to the present age, and sets all the hope upon the world to come. This is God's work. In the denominational and other 'churches', from one end of this country to the other, it is all man's work, all what they do: there is no crying, no weeping, for the work of God. No judgment of the true state. No, because these are the days when 'the judges ruled'. That is, these are the days of famine, a famine of the hearing of the words of God.

In the book of Ruth, God was witholding. He was giving no blessing. There was no rain from heaven. There was no bread in his inheritance. That is synonymous with the situation today. It is a question of how the people will respond to this. There is a famine of the word of God, and there is a famine of regeneration from God. There is plenty of 'accepting Jesus', of men making decisions. But there is little of 'it pleased God to reveal his Son in me', of God's taking hold of the soul. There is a famine, a terrible spiritual famine, a long lasting famine, a famine to which we have accustomed ourselves as though that were the normality. In the one church of God in the new testament, however, it was not so. There it was the power of God acting upon and within the congregation called 'the church which is in God the Father, and in the Lord Jesus Christ.' This is that of which there is a famine.

What is the response of man to such a famine? 'A certain man of Bethlehem-judah went to sojourn in the country of

Moab, he, and his wife, and his two sons.' The country of Moab? Actually the word rendered 'country' should read 'fields'. Evidently therefore whilst there was no yield in the land of Israel, the inheritance of the LORD and of his people, there was some sort of a yield in the fields of Moab, where neither the LORD nor Israel had any inheritance.

Thus this man turned from the LORD, refusing to bow beneath his judgments or submit to his sentence, choosing rather the pathway of superficial worldly expediency, the devices of human inventiveness and of carnal resourcefulness, to provide a counterfeit appearance of blessing, an alternative providence of man. This gave an outward show of fruition in the world, a disguise to cover up the famine by which God had judged his people, a sham façade to hide the blight of heaven from the eye of man.

My mind springs immediately to modern—and not so modern —evangelism, to the charismatic delusion, to the ecumenical movement. By these things the 'churches' have disguised from themselves, and, they hope, from the world at large, the judgment of God against them. The famine is ignored. That is exactly what is taking place. It is happening throughout professing Christianity. The frantic changes and innovations even down to 'services' and 'worship' show this. How many times have they changed their bible? They have gone from the divinely owned Authorised Version to the Revised Version, to the American Standard, the Revised Standard, to the New English Bible, till at last they arrive at a common Roman Catholic-Protestant bible on the one hand and an all-colour pop-version slang bible on the other. This is the dog returning to his vomit, and the sow that was washed to her wallowing in the mire, with a witness. Is it any wonder that there is a famine in the land, a famine of the hearing of the words of God, of fear and of reverence, of the presence of the most high God?

13

But if a man has the Spirit of God, he must worship, and worship in spirit and in truth. That is, in the Eternal Spirit, and in everlasting truth. If so, how can there be such constant changes, or indeed, any changes? Change the Eternal? Update the Everlasting? Why this instability? Because there is something in the solemnity of the Eternal that is not acceptable to the slick modern image, something awesome in the Everlasting that is uncomfortable to glib superficiality, therefore there is this constant round of fashionable change in and by the 'churches' and their 'evangelism'. They ape the world. They go down to worldly fields. It is not the blessing of the Almighty, it is the contrived window-dressing of man. It is not admitting that a famine exists, much less discerning its cause. It is a refusing to confess the displeasure of God, a running from his judgments. It is a wilful turning from the truth that God has cursed Christendom with a famine, and that he is very wroth.

Here is a man who has gone down to Moab. He is running from the spiritual reality. To deceive himself and others he puts up a pretence to avoid the truth. He goes to the world to escape from divine realities. He is really covering up the terrible fact that when he comes face to face with Almighty God, shutting out friends, relatives, home, activity, everyone and everything else, faced with the issue of his own inmost being alone with his God, he discovers that his life is radically, deeply and disastrously wrong. And if that is true of the individual, it is a thousandfold more true of the churches.

To this place the famine brings the individual soul, and it brings the gathered people. Then the famine becomes a blessing. Yet what we find today is the Elimelech spirit of yesterday. Anything but an admission of barrenness, anything but an admission of dryness, from the hand of an angry God. No, there is bread in Moab. Anything but an admission of the departure of the Lord, the quenching of the Spirit, the wrath of God. No, in the world there is 'another Jesus', there is 'another spirit', there is 'another gospel', and there is the god of another bible, and to them they will go, pastor and flock, priest and people, one and another. This is the nature of this evil generation: rather than face reality, there is a flying to the mirage. Rather than admit to no revelation of Christ, no mighty presence of God, no inwrought witness of the Holy Ghost, there is this expediency. A glossy, superficial, man-made easy believism is at hand: Moab is not far from Bethlehem-judah in time and space, a matter of hours, fifty miles. But it is an eternity away.

Where does it all lead, this expediency, this running from the presence of God, this false salvation, this religion without the glory? A full belly at first. Worldly prosperity, ease from the offence of the cross. At first. Then what? Then death. First Elimelech died, then the first born son died, and finally the last son died. None was left save Naomi, the wife of Elimelech, of all those who at the first went down to Moab for bread. It took ten years. But at the end of ten years the folly of running from the judgments of Almighty God was fully manifested. If so, then what will be the end of the present-day evangelical pretence? The evangelical 'churches' go on still with the charade, but, visibly, the machinery behind the stage is running down. Everything is declining. As the rust cankers so the gears clog, and the system grinds to a stop. Then nothing is left but death.

As things decline, attention is deflected by one activity after another, one campaign after another. One excitement after another. Like the Athenians, there must be some new thing. The mere existence of this feverish activity, this constant flurry, reveals the truth that there is no stillness in the presence of God: 'be still, and know that I am God.' The very fact of this ferment, this constant round of novelty distraction, betrays as constant a disillusionment, hurriedly shelved in favour of the new fashion, the next event to claim the attention. But all this restless searching is in Moab, in the world, to distract from the truth that the Christian, the church, the ministry should never have gone to Moab at the first. But to the flesh such stirring activity, especially of youthful freshness and enthusiasm, promises much, it augurs well. But in ten years' time? Where are the youth of ten years ago? Distracted by the youth of today? Where is the seed of ten years ago? Three parts dead. First by the wayside; then in the shallow ground; and finally choked by the world. But the seed that remains, and the only seed that remains, is that which answers to deep self-judgment, and church judgment, returning with broken-hearted contrition from the place of departure back to the land of promise.

This is what we see with Elimelech's household, which went down to Moab for bread. Where was the profit in disobedience? It led to death. For when the wheels of God's providence had turned full circle, after ten years, this Israelite woman in Moab had lost her husband and her two sons. Three parts of her house dead, and she only left alive. Save, she had acquired two Moabitish daughters-in-law, heathen idolaters forbidden to enter the congregation, a bitter encumbrance preventing her return to Israel. Bereft of her husband and her two sons, trapped by the circumstances of sinful relationships, what could she do? What was the worth at the last of that worldly expediency which had seemed so smart at the first? Doubtless, after ten years, she fully owned her folly, but it was too little, too late, and now what could she do? Where could she turn? She could do nothing. Then, affliction had wrought her perfect work, as the providence and Spirit of God combined to give forth the sweet sound of jubilee from the God of heaven to the poor afflicted woman in the land of Moab.

When a man comes to an end of himself, when he can do no more, when nothing is left, no standing, no refuge, no man, no church, no religion, but God alone, then, and not until then, will he seek the LORD with all his heart, and surely find him. It is when man is stripped of everything, devoid of all resource, nothing left to lose, that he will fall upon his face, his belly will cleave to the earth, and from the depths of his heart he will call upon his Maker and his Judge. 'I looked on my right hand, and beheld, but there was no man that would know me: refuge failed me; no man cared for my soul. I cried unto thee, O LORD: I said, Thou art my refuge.' 'For the oppression of the poor, for the sighing of the needy, now will I arise, saith the LORD.'

'To this man will I look, even to him that is poor, and of a contrite spirit, and that trembleth at my word.' What man is this? He who says 'Behold, I am vile; what shall I answer thee? I will lay mine hand upon my mouth.' 'I have heard of thee by the hearing of the ear: but now mine eye seeth thee. Wherefore I abhor myself, and repent in dust and ashes.' When a man is thus sore broken in the place of dragons, rending his heart and not his garment, when the waters come in unto his soul, when he cries from the depths of his being for the mercy of God or he perish, then the work is done.

Then it is evident that God has sent forth his light and truth to that man, God has brought him inwardly in spirit to his holy hill, to his tabernacles, and God has caused him to come to his altar, even to the altar of God. There are no exceptions to these things, no, not in all the book of God. 'Blessed is the man whom thou choosest, and causest to approach unto thee.' And how shall that choice be known to men, and that approach be evident upon earth? 'I have chosen thee in the furnace of affliction. For mine own sake, even for mine own sake, will I do it: for how should my name be polluted? and I will not give my glory to another.' By this the elect of God may be known: 'These are they which came out of great tribulation.' Only these 'wash their robes, and make them white in the blood of the Lamb.' The rest is all pretence, to which the fallen, modern, pseudo-evangelical, ecumenical church has turned, deceiving the whole world with its lightness and vanity.

17

Nevertheless, the foundation of God standeth sure, having this seal, The Lord knoweth them that are his. Everywhere and in all places there is a light, easy, slick, false pretence in the place of true religion. But the old paths are sure; the old landmarks certain. 'I will bring a third part through the fire, and will refine them as silver is refined, and will try them as gold is tried: they shall call on my name, and I will hear them: I will say, It is my people: and they shall say, The LORD is my God.'

And Naomi said, The hand of the LORD is gone out against me. Call me not Naomi, call me Mara: for the Almighty hath dealt very bitterly with me. I went out full, and the LORD hath brought me home again empty: why then call ye me Naomi, seeing the LORD hath testified against me, and the Almighty hath afflicted me? 'So Naomi returned', Ruth 1:22. And, more or less, so shall all return who are chosen and called to the kingdom, thus to enter the kingdom, as it was in the beginning, is now, and ever shall be, world without end, Amen.

II

Bread from Heaven

BOOK OF RUTH 1:6, *She had heard in the country of Moab how that the LORD had visited his people in giving them bread.*

NAOMI was sorely bereaved in Moab, and her two daughters-in-law with her. 'Then she arose with her daughters-in-law, that she might return from the country of Moab: for she had heard in the country of Moab how that the LORD had visited his people in giving them bread.' Ten fruitless years, ending in death. 'Wherefore she went forth out of the place.' She had come to full self-judgment. She had come to admit the truth.

There are people who will come so far, who will say, 'I have to admit this: the hand of the LORD has gone against me, my religion has proved to be a pretence, it has been shown to be worthless in the sight of God, a veneer of fruitless activity disguising the emptiness of all that lies within: I know that when I plunge into eternity, I must face an angry God. I admit the truth. But now I will do something about it; now I will put everything right.' This does not go to the dividing asunder of soul and spirit. Rather it is the light healing of the wound of the daughter of Jerusalem.

Naomi went deeper. She came to the place where she knew that putting anything right was quite beyond her. Put death right? Reclaim ten years? Naomi could do nothing, and, what is much more, she knew that she could do nothing. She knew that the disposal of all things was in the hands of Almighty God. And there Naomi waited, there she submitted, dependent upon the mercy of a God upon whom she had no claim, and from whom she deserved everlasting estrangement and wrath. And as with meekness she waited in this place of subjection, she heard the report, 'The Lord hath visited his people in giving them bread.'

Ten years it had taken, but now the work of God in Naomi, and towards Naomi, was complete. Now her jubilee must sound, for her warfare was accomplished. She was in a state, a permanent state, of melted submission and brokenness; her heart was fixed. Is this a ten second jaunt to the front to sign a decision card, the effect of an hour of emotional assault? Is this, 'You come; come from the back of the Hall, come from the galleries: you can find your way down the stairs to make your personal decision.' And if you do, moved as an iceberg is moved by a warm wind, to surface slush, the interior heart remaining frozen solid, the vast submerged bulk as hard as rock, what of it? Does that oblige Almighty God? Was Naomi's a ten second jaunt at the will and instigation of man, or the mighty crushing of the heart by the work of the Strength of Jacob over ten years?

When God deals with a soul, he does not cheapen the work of his hands by implying that such a soul can be dealt with in a few minutes, or in a dozen meetings, under human persuasion. The work of God is profound, because the heart is deep. And the work of God is protracted, because it is to abide for ever. Shallow foundations equal a short future. Surface work results in superficial appearances. But the work of God goes to the depths of the soul, and it results in what cannot be overthrown world without end. So it was with Naomi.

Ten years had passed, in which this woman did nothing; by the invisible and absolute commandment of God, life itself did to Naomi what nothing else, and no other person, could ever do to her. She was brought to an end of her own resources, that she might find the God of Israel her only resource. She was brought to hang in utter and absolute dependence upon the God of her salvation, as the permanent disposition of her heart. This is the kind of deep work in the sinner that caused the work of God in Great Britain to flourish in times past. This brought in the blessing, it was the blessing, that God should deign so to deal with a people. No one expects the work of God to be for so long or so deep. It is not something you can do, or that man can command, God forbid.

It is the work of God. This is the work that must be accomplished, if religion is to be genuine. Otherwise it is all froth, slick gloss, superficial reflection, surface glitter. There is a work that must precede, a work that will accomplish, and a work that shall follow. This work is the glory of God, that no flesh should boast in his presence. It is brought about by divine providence, and is wrought through the Holy Ghost. It must come from heaven, it must be of God, and it must result in soul-melted, heart-broken contrition of spirit in which the penitent is reached to the utmost depths both of being and life. This is the basis of permanence in any and all religious profession.

The woman, Naomi, had been brought to such a place of brokenness, of contrition: none but God could have performed this work. Drawn by the certain cords of providence to do what she would never have done of herself, she returned in a state of bitterness, of mourning, broken in heart and contrite in spirit, feeling herself unworthy of so much as a crumb of comfort, so much as hearing that God might have mercy upon such a wretched outcast.

Naomi did not go back for bread, although the word that there was bread in Israel was the signal for her return to her land, her God, and her people, a sign that could not be denied. Within herself, she was in such deep affliction, such bitter self-judgment, she cared not if she starved. But an invisible, almighty, invincible hand drew her, and go she must. She went back admitting the wrongness of her whole course, ten years of blasting and bitterness having wasted the choicest years of her life, leaving her both shattered and desolate. She came to judge not only the years in Moab, but the cause of the famine in Israel at the first, the rule of the judges, and her husband's disobedience in the beginning.

She came to this broken place after ten years. 'Wherefore she went forth out of the place where she was.' How was this? Because she had heard that the LORD had visited his people in giving them bread, and a strange drawing, a deep yearning, a corresponding awareness, moved her to return to Israel. It was not so much what she heard. It was not that there was a famine in Moab. It was not that she had no bread. It was not as if she cared any more about bread. It was that a wind from heaven had blown strangely over her soul, an imperceptible whisper breathed from the land of promise, and go forth she must.

Naomi was left destitute and broken, acknowledging her sin. She trembled to return, but return she must. Conflict was within her: how could she go back with the shameful evidence of threefold death and twofold disobedience? Her husband and her two sons were dead, and the living witness of their disobedience appeared in the two heathen Moabitish women whom they ought never to have married. Why go back, with such a shameful testimony? There was bread enough in Moab. But her heart was bruised and crushed, the Almighty had dealt bitterly with her, she knew it, she felt this deep work in her soul, and, conflict or no, there was that which moved strangely within her being. No one could enter into this. But the breath had come from the land of Canaan, and she had sensed it. 'The LORD is there': a word had been breathed, and she knew that the answer to her yearning lay in the land from whence she came. She wanted to get to the place from whence the word sounded, the breath came. She wanted to be under the sound. She wanted to come back.

So Naomi began the journey to Bethlehem-judah. Her two daughters-in-law, unwilling to leave her destitute, choose to accompany her, that they might care for her. Touched, Naomi turned to them and said 'Go, return each to her mother's house: the LORD deal kindly with you, as ye have dealt with the dead, and with me. The LORD grant you that ye may find rest, each of you in the house of her husband.' Then she kissed them, and they lifted up their voice, and wept, and they said unto her, 'Surely we will return with thee unto thy people.' So kind they were, refusing to leave Naomi without any to care for her, they would have left all that was dear to them to look after the stricken widow.

But Naomi said, 'Turn again, my daughters: why will ye go with me? are there yet any more sons in my womb, that they may be your husbands? Turn again, my daughters, go your way; for I am too old to have an husband. If I should say, I have hope, if I should have an husband also tonight, and should also bear sons; would ye tarry for them till they were grown? would ye stay for them from having husbands? nay, my daughters; for it grieveth me much for your sakes that the hand of the LORD is gone out against me.'

Though in her inmost heart there was shame in going back with the twofold testimony to her husband's and sons' disobedience, yet Naomi was touched at the kindness and compassion of the Moabitish women. And in dissuading them she said no more than was true. But how few can confess the LORD in such a way: 'The hand of the LORD is gone out against me.' It was the truth; it was her true testimony. How humbled, how contrite, how tender, the chastening of the LORD had left her soul: how broken before God, within herself, and to others. And yet how powerful this very testimony became.

Have you come to this place in your soul's history? the place where you can say, after ten years as it were, 'The hand of the LORD is gone out against me'? Do you say, it was unique to

Naomi? Not so: the ten is symbolic, it is a complete period, the round number of years; the chastisement is common to every child of God, of this Naomi was an example. 'For whom the LORD loveth'—mark that, whom he loveth—'he chasteneth, and scourgeth every'—observe, every—'son whom he receiveth. If ye be without chastening, whereof all are partakers, then are ye bastards and not sons.' Of this chastisement, common to all the children of God, of this kind of scourging, Naomi was the figure.

Was the hand of the LORD going out against Naomi peculiar to her, and not common to all God's people? Saith Job 'Have pity on me, have pity on me, O ye my friends; for the hand of God hath touched me.' And ye have heard of the patience of Job. Then you may gauge the length of the chastisement. David cried, 'Day and night thine hand was heavy upon me.' And again, 'Thy hand presseth me sore.' Once more, 'I am consumed by the blow of thine hand.' Isaiah also declares the word of the LORD to all Israel, saying, 'I will turn my hand upon thee, and purely purge away thy dross, and take away all thy tin: and I will restore thy judges as at the first, and thy counsellors as at the beginning: afterwards thou shalt be called, The city of righteousness, the faithful city.'

Here was this poor widow, bitter in soul and spirit. The LORD had given bread, but she had sinned, her house had sinned, amidst a sinning people. She confessed the sins of her fathers that ever a famine had come upon Israel those ten years ago, yes, but it was to herself that her deepest condemnation was reserved. She owned that the judges and rulers of Israel at that time were unrighteous, so ungodly that they had brought down the famine. The fathers had led them so wrongly, she denied their rule, it is all true, but it was nothing compared to her cutting, bitter self-judgment. 'The hand of the LORD is gone out against me.' Nothing but cursing, nothing but death: 'Turn again, my daughters.'

Turn back, turn back, for those prospects after which all mankind seeks, for which all the world looks. Turn back, turn back, to the things that nature counts dear, and that the living call life. 'Turn again, my daughters, go your way. Are there any more sons in my womb? would you tarry till they are grown?' No, go back to Moab for husbands. Of those that thus turn, the world is full. And to favour such turning, the judges of our day have brought the world into their fallen church. That is what has happened to the outward worldly church. That is what they have done to the church, to get the young people in. The force of nature is their strength, for the power of the Holy Ghost has departed. Ichabod is over all their doors. Yet the church in the beginning was spiritual. It was not devoted to worldly objectives, but to things heavenly, divine, spiritual and eternal.

'And they lifted up their voice, and wept again.' As to Orpah, she kissed her mother-in-law; but Ruth clave to her. And Naomi said to Ruth, 'Behold, thy sister-in-law is gone back unto her people, and unto her gods: return thou after thy sister-in-law.' She seeks to turn Ruth back, not bring her in. Not bring her in? But we have had generations of fast-talking American evangelists, with no more divinity than a Moabite, telling us to go to the world, to bring in the world, to be attractive to the world, and what has happened? The world has come in, and the church has quite disappeared. The daughter of Moab has come in, the daughter of Babylon has come in, pleasant enough in themselves as it appears, but, 'Turn again, my daughters'. When the church is right, when the church is reformed indeed, when the church is spiritual, there is nothing for you here: 'Turn again, my daughters.'

What is there among a true people of God for the world? The world is for 'pleasantness', for pleasure, but Naomi says, Call me no more 'Pleasant'—that is, Naomi;—call me Mara—which means, 'Bitter'—for the Almighty hath dealt very bitterly with me. God had gone forth against her; the lashes of conscience, the curse of the law, the rod of Moses, had left their indelible mark over long years. The lines were on her face, the affliction was in her eyes, the pain had marked her countenance, and the bitterness was within her soul. Call me 'Mara'. All she could show was the barrenness of heart, the weariness of the way of transgressors brought at last to repentance, and the yielded submission of one who could hold out no more against the Almighty.

You might say, What use is that? What we ought to do is show a bright, happy face, a beaming smile, a fun-loving joy, we must be attractive to the world, none of your mournful old psalms, no, a jaunty, lively Sankey chorus, the latest pop-rock christian hit, that will bring them in: the old way drives them out. Now we must 'put a little paint on your lips, dress up in the fashion, then they will see christians are not dowdy.' That's the way, says the transatlantic evangelist. And if Ruth had seen that, she would have gone back to Moab, where it originated, where it was done much better and more honestly, but she had left all that, she had left the world to go to glory, not gone to the world for a false religion. She saw what she yearned for in Naomi, and what she had come to loath is precisely what these modern liars and deceivers advocate to the destruction of millions, by their worldliness and hypocrisy in the name of 'evangelism'. This is what has laid the foundation for the charismatic delusion.

And what shall Ruth say to a person so unattractive to the young, to youth, to the world, as Naomi? She will bear this perfect sevenfold testimony to the real work of God: 'Entreat me not to leave thee, or to return from following after thee: for whither thou goest, I will go; and where thou lodgest, I will lodge: thy people shall be my people, and thy God my God: where thou diest, will I die, and there will I be buried: the LORD do so to me, and more also, if aught but death part thee and me.' What repelled the world was irresistible to the seeker. And what repelled the seeker was irresistible to the world. In Ruth it appeared. And when Naomi saw that she was steadfastly minded to go with her, then she left speaking to her.

What would people say today? Why, we must be geared to the times, tuned in, on the right wave length, we must be socially aware. Our manner must flatter the world, offence must be avoided at all costs, we must bow to the received wisdom of the judges, to the current trends, indeed our youth must be 'trendy', our women 'smart', our men must be 'yuppy', reaching for positions of influence. This is their testimony, one can be a christian, and 'normal', that is, worldly. Would such a thing draw Ruth? Those who are really seeking, as was Ruth, are puzzled, staggered and in consternation when they see this false modern expediency, because it does not agree with the witness that is within their souls. The Spirit witnesses with their spirit, but this superficial, worldly, counterfeit way is in the opposite spirit, the spirit of the world, which will quench that which is of God, it will repel that which is of the Holy Ghost, because it runs clean contrary to the anointing. The quickening witness in Ruth, however, answered to the anointing in Naomi, where the work wrought in the older woman appealed to all that was done in the soul of the younger, leading her in the way of it, showing the way beforehand, in that the same interior, spiritual work had been wrought first in the afflicted widow.

Despite all the grief, the sorrow and heartbreak, Ruth sees through to the pure gold in the heart of Naomi, she sees what she knows is of God, she perceives a divinity all of God, and she is not going to let it go. People today would not think that this would show her anything that was of God, they would think, If only Naomi had been bright and smiling, with a cultivated, light, surface charm; not too serious, a little superficial gaiety; not so depressed that she gave up the idea of another husband, or career; a little talk of Jesus, a little froth of chorus, why, that would have attracted the young woman. But it was the very opposite with Ruth.

What attracted Ruth was a middle-aged woman in widow's weeds, careless of appearance, who had seen affliction by the rod of God's wrath. Sorrow had broken her heart. 'Thy rebuke hath broken my heart.' And yet the young Moabitess saw something that caused her to forget even the thought of husband, children, home, country, nationality, culture, yes, and place of burial too, and say 'Thy people shall be my people, and thy God my God: where thou diest, will I die, and there will I be buried: the LORD do so to me, and more also, if aught but death part thee and me.' Ruth had seen the work of God, and the people in whom God wrought, whose God was the LORD, and she will not cleave to any other.

Ruth had been won by the interior work in Naomi, while she beheld her chaste conversation coupled with fear. What attracted her was the opposite to what was outward, such as painting the face, setting the hair, the wearing of adornments, jewellery, the putting on of apparel and diverse clothing and appearance—much less that suited to the opposite sex. Neither had Naomi any interest in the entertainments of Moab, the buffoonery, the music or the playing of actors: precisely the opposite. What was overwhelming in Naomi's testimony to Ruth was the hidden woman of the heart, the meek and quiet spirit, the inward adornment, the interior satisfaction with divine communion.

This drew Ruth: the modest apparel, the long hair, the covered head, the calm plainness, the shamefacedness and sobriety, the absence of artfully contrived show, of colours, scents, perfumes, cosmetics, gold, pearls, costly array. There was a resigned deep calm, an untouchable godliness in the profound depths of the soul, a silence, a subjection, that was more than words, more than appearances, it was a reality, a verity that bespoke a communion at peace with her Maker, a reaching within through time to eternity. That was what Ruth saw, and that was what Ruth wanted.

Are you like that? Is there anything of that in you? To the extent that there is something of this spirit in you, you have begun to make true progress in the things of God. Because if this is not the outward appearance of the interior work of God in those whose company you seek, or in yourself, it is not possible that the work will stand. It will be found out to be on a sandy basis at the last.

In the book of Ruth agricultural events, the agricultural year, famine, sowing, the first-ripe corn, the harvest and the gleaning, the winnowing and the gathering, are all brought into subservience to show the work of God in the redemption of his people. Ruth is a book of redemption. And the work starts, typically and anti-typically, in figure and reality, in shadow and substance, in nature and spiritually, the work starts with a famine. Without this, there is no work.

Blessed are they that hunger and thirst after righteousness. That is the start: hunger and thirst. And, if so, there is a famine. Blessed are ye that hunger now. Then the work starts with a famine. David cried out in the thirty-second psalm— quoted by Paul to show the work of justification by faith—'My moisture is turned into the drought of summer.' Then the work in David started with a spiritual famine. Jesus appealed to those in whom God had wrought such a work: If any man thirst, let him come unto me and drink. And again, to the famished he cried, I am the bread of life. The work of God in the soul of his people starts with a spiritual famine: 'Hungry and thirsty, their soul fainted in them.' Yes, but, after 'ten years', it is written 'He satisfieth the longing soul, and filleth the hungry with good things.'

Many scriptures show this in different ways. Jesus calls to him 'All ye that labour and are heavy laden', and none other. Such as have been taught of God—that is, taught the famine in their experience—the Father draws to the Son. Woe unto you that laugh now, he cries, Woe unto you that are full now. Says Mary, He hath filled the hungry with good things, and the rich he hath sent empty away. This you see in the parable

29

of the rich man and Lazarus. In every redeemed soul the LORD does such a negative, preparatory work, before that which is positive. Otherwise, the work cannot last.

This appears in the parable of the sower. Behold, a sower went forth to sow, and some fell by the wayside, some on shallow ground, some among thorns, and some seeds fell into good ground. That which fell by the wayside, the birds immediately devoured. That seed which fell on shallow ground straightway sprang up with joy, but when the sun arose, it withered, being unable to stand the heat, or to resist the drought—here were days of famine—since it had no depth of earth. That which fell among thorns lasted almost till the end, but the thorns grew stronger, and the briars grew thicker, they took the light of the sun, and the moisture from the earth, and they choked the seed. But that which fell in good ground abode for ever, bearing much fruit. Why? Why, because the ground was dug up and broken before the sower appeared on the scene, just as the soil was harrowed and raked prior to the falling of the seed upon the earth. That was the prior cause, and the sole cause of its singular fruitfulness.

Naomi signifies for all the people of God, not just for herself, she depicts in a typical way, this deep soul work, this preparatory work, in a figure the work of famine, the work that brings corruption and death fully to light in experience, the work that must precede if redemption is to be secured. This work brings a man to that degree of bitterness of soul in which he feels there is nothing in him, or from him, or for him, but corruption, decay and death. There is nothing of God in his heart, his life, or his soul, and yet he cannot and will not live without such a work. There is nothing such a man can grasp. He feels that he is so rotten and foul, and God's wrath so irrevocable, that he cannot possibly obtain mercy, that God has utterly shut him out as he deserves. He feels it deeply, and he feels the justice of it deeply. And yet he pants for God as the hart panteth for the waterbrooks, as in a dry and thirsty land. This is famine work.

But it is surely God's work. Ruth sees this in Naomi. There is a weightiness of soul in what she beholds that she knows cannot come from nature. The light and flippant sort laugh this to scorn, and suppose that religion stands in the chaff. But God says, Behold, ye despisers, and wonder, and perish: for I work a work in your days, a work which ye shall in no wise believe, though a man declare it unto you. But those whom the famine has struck believe in truth when the seed appears. For this is the solid wheat. And what is the chaff to the wheat? saith the Lord. The chaffy, light, worldly talkers go away and mock: but in that day when God raiseth the dead, and they stand before their Maker to receive their everlasting sentence, when they see those who wept in this life whilst they laughed, now laughing while they weep, aware that their weeping time hath no end, shall then lament having despised a famine work whilst there was yet time.

And now, behold this Ruth: Naomi tries to send her back, 'Go, return', she says. Ruth replies 'Entreat me not to leave thee.' Already this afflicted woman, Naomi, bears fruit. She feels destitute. She knows that she has not yet returned to the Lord, the God of Israel. She is aware that she has not yet partaken of the spiritual bread the far side Jordan. She can own the curse on all that she has done. She feels herself a seething mass of inbred corruption under the blows of God's hand. She senses that far from doing anything for God, or obtaining anything from him, she cannot expect the least crumb of mercy. She is so bitterly under the wrath of God. Yes, it may be so, but Ruth finds her attractive.

Naomi owns nothing but the work of God in bringing her to an end of herself, and in bringing this world to an end in herself. She stares death, her constant companion, in the face. Nothing remains for herself, or in the world, that she desires. 'There is none upon earth that I desire beside thee.' This produces so weighty an effect that one must stop one's mouth in the presence of such sorrow and grief, such profound divinity. This is solid work, this is real religion, and where is the hand of man in such a work? 'Cease ye from man, whose breath is in his nostrils, for wherein is he to be accounted of?' This work brings in real religion, and nothing else brings in real religion, because nothing else really gets to the bottom of the soul. All else rests upon an undisturbed, rotten foundation. The foundation must be dug up, the rottenness brought out. This is famine work, ten year work, the work that breaks down the painted sepulchre, and brings to light the rotting corpse, the work that gets to the uncleanness within the cup and platter, and disdains the mere washing of the outside. This is God's work. And where is this today?

So they two went on until they came to Bethlehem. And it came to pass, when they were come to Bethlehem, that all the city was moved about them, and they said, Is this Naomi? And she said unto them, 'Call me not Naomi—pleasant—call me Mara—bitter—for the Almighty hath dealt very bitterly with me. I went out full, and the LORD hath brought me home again empty: why then call ye me Naomi, seeing the LORD hath testified against me, and the Almighty hath afflicted me?' How true, how honest, how poignant is the testimony of God's people. Here is no put on, worked up, cosmetic testimony for some popular campaign, all shot through with dishonesty and deceit as to God's work. Here is the truth.

She went out pleasant in the judges' eyes, and she entered Moab pleasant in the world's eyes. But not in the sight of God. 'What a pleasant lady, what a dear husband, what delightful sons', so the flattery went. But now the work is done, and she is sick of flattery, she goes to the truth: Call me not Pleasant. Call me Bitter. For you see the lines, the sorrow, the marks of affliction, the change of countenance. How careful she once was to appear pleasant to man, and not a thought of God, which looketh upon the heart. Now how careful to appear pleasant to God, and how careless of man, who looketh upon the outward appearance.

Where now is this worldly pleasantness, the world's manners and flattery? what is its worth at the last? Now all Naomi's concern is to appear before God, to be counted pleasant in his sight. She had been pleasant to man and bitter before God. Now she is pleasant to God and bitter before man. Pleasant towards God? Yes, for God healeth the broken in heart. Saith David, 'A broken and a contrite heart thou wilt not despise.' 'With this man will I dwell, even with him that is of a broken and contrite spirit, that trembleth at my word.' 'The Almighty hath dealt very bitterly with me. I went out full, but the LORD hath brought me home again empty.' That is it, The LORD hath brought me home. Then her coming home was his doing. As to the emptiness, 'Why call ye me pleasant, seeing the LORD hath testified against me?' Yes, but whom the LORD loveth he chasteneth. None other. Then, he took pleasure in the work of his own hands. Pleasant towards God.

Is this exclusive to Naomi? is this her case alone? No, it is the case with every sinner, more or less, whom the LORD brings to himself. If the man or woman whom the LORD will chasten be found in some congregation or another, first the famine will be felt, though not by them. The solitary chastened soul will soon discover the congregation's bread to be but the husks on which the swine feed, it is but the dry chaffy castings of the dead letter. A deep seated hungering and thirsting will soon set apart the poor soul. The rest will feel that the hand of the LORD has gone out against him, Job's comforters will arise, and full many false physicians, especially if the man has any substance. But it will avail them nothing. God is at work, and who can let it?

What had Naomi done? She had done nothing. Of herself, she had not even gone down to Moab. Her husband had taken her. It was all in the determinate counsel and fore-knowledge of God, and so is redemption. What can I do? What can you do? We can do nothing. Progressively evangel-icalism has drifted upon a series of vast popular evangelistic waves over the past century and a half which have swept away the denominations and the so-called 'evangelicals' in the state churches, till, hopelessly adrift on a sea of error, they proclaim, We do everything. Then God does nothing. This is the real apostasy. It is antichrist. It has resulted in the charismatic floods which have let in popery. There will be no repentance or recovery from this. It is a judgment. It is God's sent delusion. The word is, 'Come out of her, my people', and happy is that Noah or Lot who escapes the city of destruction. Perhaps the worst failure, and the most disappointing— because it showed the greater promise—is that of Brethrenism. But from the very start they embraced easy-believism, just as from the beginning they flattered popery and the Eastern church, telling us of all the 'simple believers' among these corrupt and apostate systems. Both J.N. Darby and W. Kelly stand guilty of this miserable deception. So obsessed were they with forming the outward semblance which they said showed the unity of the body of Christ, that in their infatuation they walked with multitudes who were not of that body. The word is, Come out of her, my people. And this word must and will reach those who hunger and thirst under the famine which the apostate and antichristian profession calls, fulness of bread.

'What can we do?' they cry. We can do nothing. Salvation belongeth unto the LORD. It is all of God. 'You place it beyond our reach', they complain. It is beyond our reach. But we are not beyond his reach who declares, 'I will have mercy upon whom I will have mercy.' Next they cry, 'Who then can be saved?' 'With man it is impossible'; saith Jesus in answer to this very question, 'but with God all things are possible.' And the possibility starts with a famine.

III

The Beginning of Barley Harvest

BOOK OF RUTH 1:22, *And they came to Bethlehem in the beginning of barley harvest.*

THERE is a time appointed for Zion, a time when her afflictions cease, her calamities pass, when her travail has an expected end. Then the time of barrenness is over, and they cry over her with joy 'Rejoice, O barren, thou that didst not bear; break forth into singing, and cry aloud, thou that didst not travail with child.' Her weeping time is over, and the time of rejoicing is come. The hungering and the thirsting is past, and the LORD shall satisfy her with good things. 'So Naomi returned, and Ruth the Moabitess, her daughter-in-law, with her, which returned out of the country of Moab: and they came to Bethlehem in the beginning of barley harvest', Ruth 1:22.

Now the beginning of barley harvest is just after the passover. If so, Naomi and Ruth were brought back—after ten years— to a passover completed. It was finished, and the harvest was in view. The barley harvest, as it were, appeared in the good of the passover having been sacrificed. The harvest was to be brought home in the light of the sprinkling of the blood of the lamb, which preceded the reaping. The truth of this, and its spiritual significance, brought before the reader of the book of Ruth by the Holy Ghost, must now be opened and expounded in the following pages.

Firstly it is to be shown that 'the beginning of barley harvest' was in fact just after the passover. The significance of the passover itself is clear: it is the time appointed for the death of Christ, 'the Lamb slain from the foundation of the world',

Rev. 13:8, as it is written, I Cor. 5:7, 'For even Christ our passover is sacrificed for us.' Yes, but how do we know that this sacrifice, or the type of the sacrifice in the passover lamb, preceded the gathering of the barley harvest? Naomi may have returned 'in the beginning of barley harvest', but how can we show that this was just after the slaying and eating of the passover?

Exodus 23:14,15 records, 'Three times thou shalt keep a feast unto me in the year. Thou shalt keep the feast of un-leavened bread'—that was the first feast, at the passover, the first feast of the agricultural year—'thou shalt eat unleavened bread seven days, as I commanded thee, in the time appointed of the month Abib; for in it thou camest out from Egypt.' Here is the time of the feast of unleavened bread, immed-iately following the passover, it is the time 'appointed of the month Abib', in terms of agriculture, each year. Moreover, the time is fixed in terms of history, historically they were to connect the feast with a past event: 'for in it'—the month Abib—'thou camest out from Egypt.'

When was this month 'Abib', and what does the word mean? The word, referring to corn, means matured or grown in the ear. It is the 'ear' month, the month 'Abib', because the ears of barley were formed; though green, they had come to full ear. As to the time, Israel was commanded 'Observe the month Abib, and keep the passover unto the LORD thy God: for in the month Abib'—the first month—'the LORD thy God brought thee forth out of Egypt by night', Deut. 16:1. It is the 'ear' month because it is the month of the ripening of the first harvest. Then, it is the beginning of barley harvest. The word 'Abib', in relation to corn, indicates the coming to fruition, the corn is in the ear, it is the 'ear' month, the month of the first harvest, that is, the barley harvest. Israel kept the passover in the month Abib, the month in which the barley was formed, but not quite ripe, in the ear. The beginning of barley harvest therefore indicates the passover just com-pleted, because the passover is reckoned from the start of the month Abib. It is at the commencement of Abib that the harvest is in the ear, the fourteenth day is that of the passover, and the following days of that month are those in which the barley begins to be harvested.

Exodus 13:4 records 'This day'—the passover—'came ye out in the month Abib.' Came ye out? Yes, from Egypt. Prior to that coming out the plagues had fallen on Egypt. Ten plagues. A complete number. With the tenth plague—the slaying of the firstborn—the LORD, who had hardened Pharaoh's heart hitherto, brought Israel out of the land of Egypt. Before the Exodus, however, the seventh plague had fallen with great severity: dreadful thunder and hail, with fire running along the ground, as the LORD rained great hailstones upon the land of Egypt. 'The flax and the barley'—mark that, the barley—'was smitten: for the barley was in the ear', Ex. 9:31. Because of the barley being in the ear, the month was called Abib. In it, after three more plagues, that is, after the passover, Israel came out of Egypt.

It was the month in which the green barley was formed in the ear, the barley was mature, but not yet ripe. This accorded with the law of the firstfruits, Leviticus 2:14, 'Thou shalt offer for the meat offering of thy firstfruits green ears of corn dried by the fire, even corn beaten out of full ears.' Such was the condition of the barley when Naomi and Ruth came to Bethlehem 'in the beginning of barley harvest', Ruth 1:22, a condition which obtained following the slaying of the passover lamb.

Naomi's experience over ten years corresponded experimentally with the ten plagues, commemorated in Israel over the first ten days of the month Abib. But the commemoration of the ten plagues in the first ten days of the month was a mere outward ceremony, a form, an ordinance. It could not bring into the inward experience. However, Naomi had been brought into the inward experience, she had been taken off

37

the outward form and been brought into the inward reality, out of the dead letter into the spiritual consciousness of the wrath of God going forth against the whole of mankind, from which nothing but the sprinkled blood of the lamb was a shelter. That marked the true Israelite, the Israelite indeed. These felt their deserts under the plagues, they felt the judgment of God, they afflicted their souls under the wrath of God, they fled from the wrath to come. That was what led the true Israelites to the blood of the lamb, and that was what the ten years of affliction had taught Naomi.

The passover was to be eaten with bitter herbs, and the experience of bitterness over ten years was precisely the lesson impressed upon Naomi. She named herself 'Bitter' in consequence. 'Call me not Naomi, call me Mara: for the Almighty hath dealt very bitterly with me.' Here she is a figure of the child of God, although the superficial, empty, modern evangelicals would never admit this, for it was never their experience. But it is our experience, shown forth in Naomi, whose passover was eaten with bitter herbs not in form only, not in the letter merely, not simply in traditional ceremony, but in reality. So is Christ our passover, when assimilated by the true children of God, as opposed to the chaffy, dead-letter professors, who know nothing of keeping the reality of the feast, although each 'Lord's day morning' they religiously maintain the form, as they think.

Naomi was taught of God the experience. The 'bitter' herbs signified to her the bitter experience of the work of God in her soul in answer to the plagues that fell, which she knew she deserved every whit as much as the Egyptians. The curse of God had been on her soul, the wrath of God had gone forth against her, the loathsomeness of her sin had brought down the judgment of heaven, and the LORD God had dealt very bitterly with her, and this she had experienced for 'ten days'— or rather ten years—in her interior experience. This was the reality of the bitter herbs, without which the passover was nullified and inappropriate to the partaker.

How little there is today of this brokenness, this coming to an end, this bitterness, this being brought to eat of the flesh of the Son of man and to drink his blood. The saviour himself affirms these words, so tremendously vital is it to come into that by which God leads and draws the soul into the spiritual knowledge of Christ. When a man 'claims' this or that for himself about salvation from the Almighty, and picks up a text here and there, and copies or reiterates someone else's experience, or is worked up emotionally by others, or 'thinks things through' intellectually, the work can never stand, it cannot reach to the depths wrought by the living God. But when 'ten days'—or rather ten years—precede being brought to the Lamb of God, then the soul comes to an end of itself, the depths are broken up, the truth is powerfully inwrought, the heart is broken, the spirit made contrite, a mighty change is effected, there is the taste of bitter herbs to the Lamb. What a different thing this is from all that man can do. This is the work of God.

This is the work that had been wrought in Naomi, and over these ten years there was that in her which signified what takes place in all regenerate souls, as opposed to the flippant, light, spurious converts of these latter days. Ten years had passed before there was wrought a complete sense of the sinfulness of sin, a fear of the wrath to come, a profound reverence for the majesty and holiness of God, a trembling under the divine judgments. No religion is of any worth without this prior work. Without this the soul cannot and will not stand. In itself this does not save, but there is no true and lasting salvation without it. Truly nothing but the revelation of the love of Christ can save, but if the love of Christ is sown on stony or shallow ground, then the seed will and must perish. This is your teaching. This is the teaching of the great divines throughout the history of the church. This is the teaching from which, over something like the last century and a half, evangelicalism has departed in favour of light and superficial Americanised 'evangelism'.

If we are to see any kind of reviving, or reformation, or restoration, a returning to apostolic simplicity, power and life, the generation that now rules, even as their fathers ruled before them, must go, and a new generation must take their place. That is the principle behind the truth supernaturally manifested at the conclusion of Mark, the book of the servant and service of God, where, within the tomb, a radiant young man appeared, clothed in a long white garment. The women looked into the tomb, but Jesus had gone; sitting in his place they saw the young man in bright raiment. That is what is brought in for divine service by Christ risen. All the flattery, the man pleasing, the looking sideways at the evangelical party line, all is utterly excluded. The young man is not holding the hand of some aged Pharisee. He is not run by a committee. He is not the paid servant of the church. He is radiantly at rest in the place of the passover Lamb, and in the power of his resurrection. He does not need the support of man, morally or otherwise, he fears God alone. That is God's work. That is the work which has been withdrawn from the past generations. Mark these words, for the glory is departed. But God may yet be entreated of a heart-broken, penitent people, as in the days of Ruth, or in the times of Malachi.

Despite all appearances, despite her own first conclusions, the Almighty would have mercy upon Naomi. He was entreated of her. She came back to the passover, and God brought her to taste, to experience, to eat of that passover lamb, to be sheltered beneath the precious blood upon the lintel and the door posts. Jesus was indeed objectively the Lamb of God which taketh away the sin—not sins—of the world, but to Naomi, who ate of that flesh and who drank of that blood, he was infinitely more subjective, more inward, more interior, than the world could ever imagine. That night, loins girded, feet shod, staff in hand, Exodus 12:11, as a pilgrim she experienced a vital union, a real communion with the slain Lamb, and, withal, the taste of bitter herbs.

The world's religion knows nothing of this, and never will know anything of it. But God brought Naomi to the substance of true religion, and, of that, she stands a figure till the end of time. 'Except ye eat the flesh of the Son of man, and drink his blood, ye have no life in you.' The passover was concluded, Naomi had found life. And every step of the work, every moment of the working was of God. 'I the LORD do keep it; I will water it every moment: lest any hurt it, I will keep it night and day.' All was of God, in bringing Naomi to the Lamb of God, in bringing the Lamb of God to Naomi, and in her eating the passover as a pilgrim, a stranger on the earth.

Moses commanded in the law that after the passover there should follow other yearly feasts to the LORD, the next commencing immediately after the slaying of the lamb, with other feasts numbered from that which was in 'the beginning of months'. All the feasts were annual, synchronized with the agricultural cycle of the people and of the land. Each one of the feasts had great spiritual and typical significance. In fact the entire week following the passover was an holy convocation, named the feast of unleavened bread. Immediately the passover was concluded, 'In the first day ye shall have an holy convocation' until the seventh day. 'When ye be come into the land which I give unto you, and shall reap the harvest thereof, then ye shall bring a sheaf of the firstfruits of your harvest unto the priest: and he shall wave the sheaf before the LORD, to be accepted for you: on the morrow after the sabbath the priest shall wave it', Lev. 23:10,11.

The priest shall wave the sheaf? What sheaf? The sheaf made up 'of the firstfruits of your harvest', Lev. 23:10. At the time of the passover, when the barley was 'in the ear', some of the corn was already ripened, there were those stalks which matured first, before the main harvest. The fields were covered with the green ears of standing corn, the promise of harvest in the early part of the month Abib. However some heads of barley were even now yellowing, and it was these that were called the firstfruits. Israel was to go into the field to cut off such stalks, those conspicuously yellow, making up enough to bind into a sheaf, the 'first-ripe sheaf', this they were to bring to the priest, immediately after the passover. This was the sheaf that was waved before the LORD 'on the morrow after the sabbath.' From the waving of this sheaf Israel counted fifty days, or a cycle of seven complete sabbaths. On the fiftieth day, yet another feast had its commencement, the whole harvest having been gathered in during the interval. This latter feast was called the feast of Pentecost, 'Pentecost' indicating 'fifty'. This signified the conclusion of the fifty day period which was counted from the sabbath immediately following the passover. Whence it is evident that one feast followed on from the other, all the feasts were intimately and closely linked, and, of course, all commenced with 'the beginning of barley harvest', that is, the binding of the first-ripe sheaf.

This was the very time in which Naomi and Ruth came to Bethlehem. Naomi felt that she could not hope for mercy. The Holy One of Israel would not so much as look at her. She thought herself too abominable and loathsome, too openly and visibly under the curse, for any pity or compassion from him whom she had provoked so grievously, whose wrath had gone forth so evidently against her. Yet at least she could return to the land in which God's presence was made known, to which his dealings pertained. She indicated to Ruth, however, that no blessing, nothing but bitterness, could come from association with her, urging the young woman on this account to return to Moab. But Ruth, though, like Naomi, from far off, sought the same things. Such was the pity of the LORD— although neither woman was aware of it—that even with the seeking they had begun spiritually to partake of the true passover. Or ever they were aware, their sins had been covered by the blood of the Lamb. And now, in the beginning of barley harvest, they beheld the waving of the first-ripe sheaf.

What did this mean? Of what was the sheaf typical? Why was it waved? Why on the morrow after the sabbath? What was the significance of these events? First one must grasp the significance of the term 'the morrow after the sabbath'. This refers to the first day of the week. The sabbath being ended, dawn breaks 'towards the first day of the week'. At such an early hour, centuries after Naomi, certain women 'came to the tomb'. But the stone had been rolled away, and an angel sat upon the stone. The mighty angel announced on the first day of the week the resurrection from the dead of him who had been put to death three days before 'when they killed the passover'. But they had killed that passover, whom countless lambs had typified in past millennia. They had slain Jesus, the Lamb of God, which taketh away the sin of the world, and now, three days later, on the morrow after the sabbath, the first day of the week, he was risen from the dead. On that day the priest performed the ritual waving of the first-ripe sheaf. But the ritual was finished, for Christ the firstfruits was risen from the dead.

Wherefore Christ became the firstfruits of them that slept, I Cor. 15:20. He was the first-ripe sheaf. Cut off by death, but raised from the dead, the firstborn from the dead, the first-born of the new creation, he appears as the heavenly man, the man not connected with the old world or associated with the present earth. Here was the promise of the whole harvest, won by his death, waved towards heaven in a figure. And if the firstfruit be holy, the lump shall be holy, Rom. 11:16. He had died for a people whom he justified by his blood, through death to be as assured of the resurrection in him, as the harvest was assured in the waved first-ripe sheaf. 'Christ the firstfruits; afterward they that are Christ's at his coming', I Cor. 15:23.

And if raised from the dead after the sabbath, 'the sabbath being ended', this indicates that following the death of Christ in the passover, the sabbath and all that it stood for had passed away, everlasting rest had been brought in, the type had ended. 'My Father worketh hitherto, and I work'—on the sabbath—but no more: rest, and everlasting rest, had been achieved by the blood of Christ. The sabbath stood for God's rest in the old creation, but it typified a coming ever-lasting sabbath in the new creation. The sabbath indicated God's rest in the first man Adam, but it typified God's rest in the second man Christ. The sabbath indicated God's dealing with this present world and the kingdoms of the world, in this age, but it typified God's dealing with the world to come, and the kingdom of heaven in the everlasting glory. The sabbath indicated God's relationship with men under the law, but it typified God's relationship in his own Son without the law. All that had been indicated for the time then present passed away when the sheaf was raised. All that the sabbath typified was brought to pass with the fulfilment of the waving of the first-ripe sheaf. 'The morrow after the sabbath the priest shall wave it.'

Hence the reckoning no longer concerned the old world, the first Adam, the old man, the old law, the legal rule, all concerned Christ crucified, Christ risen, the world to come, the last Adam, the second man, the gospel, the baptism of the Holy Ghost, everything was to be reckoned, for perfect rest—the sabbath of sabbaths, seven sabbaths—to the day of Pentecost from the resurrection of Christ. The sabbath and all that it stood for was over, the testimony was to the risen Son, of whom the waved first-ripe sheaf on the first day of the week was the type: 'Christ the firstfruits'. It is a figure of Christ, our firstfruits, who, as our passover, had been sacri-ficed for us, and in being sacrificed for us had taken away sin, death, the condemnation of the law, the sentence of the law, the rule of the law, the first man, our old man, the first world, the old world, time, the earth, yea, the very elements consti-tuting this corruptible creation. Now is Christ risen from the dead, and become the firstfruits of them that slept. He was raised from the dead by the glory of the Father on the morrow after the sabbath, and he was presented to God in resurrection glory in the priestly praise of his heavenly people, yes, and is so still: 'O thou that inhabitest the praises of Israel.'

The morrow after the sabbath was the day of resurrection, Mt. 28:1, Mk. 16:1, Lk. 24:1. The wave sheaf indicated Christ risen. The Sun of righteousness arose to lighten the temple by way of the east. The resurrection set forth a new day, the Sun being in the heavens, Psalm 19:4-7. A new day, a new creation, a new heavens, a new earth, a new man, and a new harvest, according to the sowing of his own seed, assured by the raising up of the wave sheaf of the firstfruits. 'He that goeth forth and weepeth, bearing precious seed, shall doubtless come again with rejoicing, bringing his sheaves with him.' When the corn of wheat fell into the ground, and died, justification was obtained for all the seed. When Christ our passover was sacrificed for all the elect seed, the sabbath and all that it stood for was over. When Christ the firstfruits was 'waved' towards heaven, evident token before God of the resurrection from the dead, full of heavenly fruit, certain harbinger of the full harvest, when he was waved, I say, all the seed was waved in him. From this, Israel was to reckon. And, into the spiritual good of such heavenly food, Naomi and Ruth came, 'At the beginning of barley harvest.'

Deuteronomy 16:9 supplies yet another passage in which the first-ripe sheaf is seen as typifying and foreshadowing Christ and the gospel for the faith of Israel: 'Seven weeks shalt thou number unto thee: begin to number the seven weeks from such time as thou beginnest to put the sickle to the corn.' That was when the first-ripe sheaf was cut. This signifies the firstfruits of the harvest which God would give by Jesus Christ. He who discerned the significance of the first sheaf, would also perceive the significance of the harvest: it appears that those for whom Christ died are risen with him and numbered with him by faith of the operation of God. 'Seven weeks shalt thou number unto thee.' All Naomi's and Ruth's numberings were from this, the beginning of barley harvest, 'as thou beginnest to put the sickle to the corn.'

It is a question of numbering: 'thou shalt number unto thee.' Faith numbers, or reckons—faith counts—from a certain event, and by faith the life is lived from that event after which everything is reckoned, for, 'The just shall live by faith'. The reckoning of faith is from the waving of the sheaf 'on the morrow after the sabbath'. That is, the first day of the week. On that day, 'In the end of the sabbath, as it began to dawn toward the first day of the week, came Mary Magdalene and the other Mary to see the sepulchre. And, behold, there was a great earthquake: for the angel of the Lord descended from heaven, and came and rolled back the stone from the door, and sat upon it. His countenance was like lightning, and his raiment white as snow: and for fear of him the keepers did shake, and became as dead men. And the angel answered and said unto the women, Fear not ye: for I know that ye seek Jesus, which was crucified. He is not here: for he is risen.'

From this, the saints number. This is the day, the first day, the morrow after the sabbath, the day of the waving of the first-ripe sheaf, the resurrection day, from which all is to be reckoned, or counted. What is to be reckoned? That Christ is not here: that he has been lifted up in resurrection from the earth: that he is the firstfruits of that creation which is heavenly, that which comes down from God out of heaven. That is, of the church, the heavenly bride taken out of the side of Christ in the deep sleep of his death, that spiritual help meet for the heavenly man. The two Marys depict this. They are the twofold witness of the bride of Christ. Both bear the name Mary: 'Mara'. They have been taught of God, they see the vision. And they reckon from it. And so does that church which they represent.

Reckon from what? From the lifting up of Christ in resurrection. The angel who gave the law rolled away the stone of the law, and rested thereon. The law was given by the disposition of angels, it was ordained by angels and written upon tables of stone. Here the angel is seated, at rest, on the stone. Death has satisfied the old, legal, angelic ministration, the ministration of death, cursing, and condemnation. The administrators, the angels, see that the death of Christ has magnified the law and made it honourable, fulfilling its every demand. There is no reckoning from the law, but there is reckoning from the law having been fully met, lawfully satisfied, by the death of Christ, the angels themselves being witness.

Then who are these who tell us that Christians are under the law as a rule of life? These are they that cannot believe in his death, cannot number from his resurrection, and cannot perceive the revelation of the mystery, because they were never taught of God under the law, nor delivered from the law by grace in the gospel. Had they been delivered they would not contradict the gospel. But the church—signified by 'Mara'—has been taught of God under the law, the bride of Christ has been through the bitter experience, for ten years as it were, and she knows by revelation that she has become dead to the law by the body of Christ. Such a bride is set forth by the two Marys, to whom is revealed the heavenly vision, and, not being disobedient thereto, they begin to number 'from the beginning of barley harvest'.

Taught by grace, enlightened by revelation, led into all truth, the bride perceives the heavenly mystery. She sees the end of sin, the end of the law, the end of the old man, the end of the first creation; she reckons from justifying righteousness, from the life-giving Spirit, from the heavenly man, from the evangel, from a new creation. This is the reckoning of faith, and such numbering brings in righteousness, it brings in life, it brings in the Spirit, it brings in the glory, and it brings in the blessed hope. That is the way in which faith will, and faith must reckon. If reckoned, or numbered, aright, in terms of perfect rest—typically, seven sabbaths—won through death, then the bride will see herself—though called 'Mara'—at rest in him, yea, risen in him, and shall assuredly receive the witness of the Spirit to the place of the spouse of Christ. This is precisely the significance of the feast of Pentecost, to which the seven sabbaths led and pointed. It is the testimony of the

Spirit, sent down from the risen and ascended firstfruits, to the whole harvest, of the heavenly place gained for the bride through death and in resurrection. This is the place of the church, the true church, and it is brought to pass experimentally as faith numbers from the passover on through the feast of unleavened bread to the place of perfect rest at the time when the day of Pentecost has fully come.

But this is not the reckoning of Christendom, nor of that which the world at the present day supposes to be the church. The greater part of Christendom numbers from the coming of the Son of God into the world, from his incarnation, from the birth of Jesus Christ. That is, his life is regarded as the example, and his teaching as exemplary. The world agrees with this, numbering time itself from the advent of Christ, the terms A.D. or B.C. dividing time by the watershed of the incarnation. The 'year of our Lord', anno Domini, the advent, is made that point from which the world reckons, as a result of its having been 'christianised' by the church, so-called. The counting of Christ's life as an objective ideal, a standard set before man and humanity to try and copy, is really that by which the outward church would bind the consciences of men, whilst dazzling their superstitious eyes with a show of mediaeval dress, priestcraft, ceremony and tradition. This is counting from Jesus' advent, and the ancient temple form, with a witness, but, saith the God of Israel, 'Begin to number from such time as thou puttest the sickle to the corn.'

What the professing church, as it is called, declares by this numbering, or reckoning, from the birth and subsequent life of Christ, is that Jesus came into the world in order to improve the quality of mankind, to elevate humanity, to uplift society, as a result of his teaching and example. He came—by his exemplary life and death—to make the world a better place: that was the result of his—ineffectual—passage through this world. Still, for all the sad failure, the frustration, we must 'try his works to do', we must be 'Christ-like', we must follow his standard, we must study his example, his humanity, his compassion, and do our best, aided by the 'church', to which, consequently, it would be helpful to give our support.

But what is the good of an example to fallen man? What is the good of enslaved and blinded sinners copying a perfect humanity? What is the use of 'do-gooding' and false charity to heathen sunk in idolatry and death? Man needs redemption. Sinners need salvation. Regeneration, not example, is required. And redemption, salvation, regeneration, are not counted from the advent of Christ in the experience of the regenerate, but from 'Such time as thou beginnest to put the sickle to the corn.'

Oh, but, say the droves of parasitical priests, Oh, pontificates the 'church', but by his exemplary loving compassion, by his unselfishness, by his unworldliness, by the gentle non-resistance of his death, by the disinterested benevolence of his life, Jesus Christ is our example. We must try; we shall fail; but if we hold his objective life, his history, before us, as taught and set forth by the church in her ministry and sacraments, we shall fail gracefully. Yet why do these teachers fail themselves even so much as to try for their own part? Because they know nothing of redemption, nothing of salvation, and because they are not regenerate. Were they, they would not point men to a path of hopeless frustration, copying what they have neither nature, strength, nor life to follow. As well preach to the graves as tell fallen and lost humanity to follow the teachings of Christ in the days of his flesh.

The spiritual Israel of God, the true church, numbers from the resurrection of Jesus Christ from the dead, from the declaration of the Son of God with power, according to the spirit of holiness, by the resurrection from the dead. The church reckons from full justification wrought, from free redemption purchased, from unconditional salvation established, from the power of his resurrection, from the baptism of the Holy Ghost. I say, spiritual Israel counts from the risen, glorified Son of God, from Jesus Christ on high, from five glorified scars in his heavenly body, reckoning from the life that streams from the ascended Son in the excellent glory, life which fills and sustains the church of the living God. What a difference from an artificially contrived and dead-letter example, in a petrified ceremonial 'church', presided over by greedy priests that can never have enough, Isa. 56:9-12.

The traditional, the State, the formal churches, as they are called, think that Christ came into the world to make the world better, by his example and teaching, although after two thousand years of this example and teaching, a bloated, rich, depraved and corrupt 'church', presumes that its function is to declare this example to mankind. But after two thousand years the world is nothing bettered, but rather made worse. Is the world better now than it was then, or worse? Who follows this example? The 'Christian' West? Does the 'church', pontificating on what men and the world should do, follow his example? Does the Vatican bank? Does the property board of the Church of England? Do the clerics? One sees more vaunted glory, pomp and circumstance, airs and graces, robes and titles, on the part of the 'church', than ever there was on the part of those whom they have the impertinence to urge to follow Christ's example.

Hypocrites! That which is highly esteemed among men is abomination in the sight of God. How can they believe, which receive honour one from another—Master, Master; Reverend, Reverend; Pastor, Pastor; Doctor, Doctor; B.D., D.D., M.Th., all worldly honours which they have invented, contrary to the apostolic rule, contrary to the law of Christ—thus despising the honour that cometh from God only. Hypocrites! They are a standing illustration of the truth that fallen nature is incapable of following a good example. 'How to perform that which is good I find not', Rom. 7:18. This is the 'bitter' discovery, the 'ten years' discovery, upon which all vital and inward Christian experience is founded. And what do the clergy know of that? Nothing at all. Nor do any others of their sort, who pretend to follow an example which they know in their heart they can never keep.

There is another class of religious persons who fall short of reckoning aright, who do not 'number from such time as thou beginnest to put the sickle to the corn'. It is not that they number from the incarnation, from the example and life of Christ, no, they are the 'evangelical' party, they number from his death. They reckon from the cross. They are not easily detected, they deceive multitudes, they appear to be so biblical. But theirs is a killing ministry, they are of the dead letter that killeth. They reckon from the cross, but they know nothing of the power of his resurrection. They intellectualise or sentimentalise about 'the Lord's death, brother', especially on what they call 'Lord's day morning', but they are utterly devoid of a living ministry. They know nothing of 'with great power gave the apostles witness to the resurrection from the dead', no, their religion never reaches to the resurrection, never reaches to the ascension, never reaches to Pentecost, it is all dead men muttering about an objective historical event that occurred two thousand years ago.

Such as these fetch all their religion from the Bible, but none from the living God. All from history, but none from life. All from eyesight, but nothing from revelation. All from the Gospel Hall, but not a word from heaven. They themselves, unregenerate and void of the power and indwelling of the Holy Ghost, they themselves, I say, provide the strength of their religion: what do they know of 'Mara', or of 'ten years'? Nothing whatever. What do they know of 'Ye have an unction from the Holy One, and know all things', or, 'The anointing which ye have received of him abideth in you, and ye need not that any man teach you'? They have no anointing, but they have the Bible, brother—or at least, some corrupt version of it—and what do they need with anointings? They suppose that they have the cross, they reckon they have the blood, they think that they have the Lord's table. Not so: they have the narrative of the cross, they have texts on the blood, and they have their own table. But they are all as dead men, with a dead religion, with an objective, traditional system held in the flesh. And the reason is, they do not, and in their system they cannot 'reckon from such time as thou beginnest to put the sickle to the corn'. Reckon, that is, until the day of Pentecost be fully come, when 'there came a sound from heaven as of a rushing mighty wind, and it filled all the house where they were sitting. And they were all filled with the Holy Ghost.'

However the true Israel of God, all of whom have been taught of God—as it is written, 'They shall be all taught of God'—pass through the years of 'Mara' experience, in consequence of which they are brought to an end of themselves, they are made poor in spirit, they mourn, they are broken-hearted, and contrite in spirit. This the psalmist describes, saying 'Blessed is the man whom thou chastenest, O Lord, and teachest out of thy law.' This teaching, typically, is far off from Israel, in Moab, before the knowledge of Christ, but necessarily preceding it. Indeed, this divine teaching, this chastisement, constitutes the only way to Christ, the only condition upon which he is truly revealed, and to which he is really made known, as he himself says, 'Every man therefore that hath heard, and hath learned of the Father, cometh unto me.' As to these, he declares, 'All that the Father giveth me shall come to me; and him that cometh to me I will in no wise cast out', John 6:37,45.

But to the people who are satisfied with a form of religion out of the dead letter, who search the scriptures on the mistaken supposition that in them these may find life, to such, I say, the risen, anointed, ascended, baptising, saviour saith, 'Ye shall seek me, and shall not find me, and where I am,

thither ye cannot come', John 7:34. However, all the elect
seed of God, all that are taught of God in far off Moab, every
poor outcast and mourner, having first endured the chastening of the LORD, having been taught of the Father, shall
surely come to Christ 'In the beginning of barley harvest'.

In the land of promise they shall see the waving of the first-
ripe sheaf. And if so, they shall reckon themselves to be of
that seed, and assured of the harvest. How can they so reckon?
How can it be proved that all the people of God are seen in
that one small wave sheaf? How is it possible? By faith. 'There
came a man from Baal-shalisha, and brought the man of God
bread of the firstfruits, twenty loaves of barley, and full ears
of corn in the husk thereof. And he said, Give unto the
people, that they may eat. And his servitor said, What,
should I set this before an hundred men?' It was far too little,
it was ridiculous, it would not feed a fraction of that number.
How can a multitude be satisfied when there is not enough
barley bread to feed a few? 'He said again, Give the people,
that they may eat: for thus saith the LORD, They shall eat,
and shall leave thereof. So he set it before them, and they did
eat, and left thereof, according to the word of the LORD',
II Kings 4. For by faith all things are possible. And to those
taught of the Father, Christ 'waved' as the firstfruits in the
resurrection, all righteousness fulfilled, is the reckoning that
leads to the fulness of Pentecost, because all the harvest is
seen in the first-ripe sheaf. When that reckoning was fulfilled,
'they were all filled with the Holy Ghost'.

Once more: It is abundantly clear that when Christ rose,
all his people rose in him. When he presented himself before
God, every one of them was presented before God in him, his
God their God, his Father their Father, his place their place,
his blessing their blessing, the measure of the Spirit upon
him, the measure of the Spirit upon them. Pentecost showed
the accuracy of the numbering, the correctness of such counting. The Spirit that proceeded from him, filled them. They

were in him, and he was in them. And this was because of the reality reckoned from the resurrection from the dead, when all the elect, redeemed, justified, yea, glorified 'harvest' was seen in the firstfruits of them that slept. This is what was determined when he appeared before God on their behalf, with every enemy slain, every foe defeated, Crying, 'O death, where is thy sting? O grave, where is thy victory? Death is swallowed up in victory.'

Thus the first-ripe barley sheaf was both typified and fulfilled. All the seed appeared in him, and he appeared in all the seed. 'There is a lad here, which hath five barley loaves, and two small fishes: but what are they among so many?' And what is one small barley sheaf, that it should contain all the elect people of God, all the seed of God, securing for them the earnest of their inheritance, the baptism of the Spirit on the day of Pentecost, as well the everlasting glory of the resurrection from the dead in the world to come? How can so much, for such multitudes, be absolutely, irrevocably, displayed and secured in one small sheaf, that such vast provision can be reckoned with certainty from the waving of that sheaf?

And Jesus said, Make the men sit down. Here is the rest of faith. The company reposed at the command of Christ: they are sitting at rest under his word; this is reckoning by faith indeed. Here is the sabbath of sabbaths. So the men sat down, in number about five thousand. 'And Jesus took the loaves; and when he had given thanks, he distributed to his disciples, and the disciples to them that were set down; and likewise of the fishes, as much as they would. And they were all filled.' What? Five thousand men from five barley loaves? Yes, and when the doctrine of the grace of Christ is brought home in the power and anointing of the Holy Ghost, so that men reckon from it, and sit down under it, and Christ's ministers in the apostolic gospel distribute it to those who are in the rest of God by faith, yes, they will and they must be filled. 'And they were all filled with the Holy Ghost.'

This is that experimental union with Christ which the people of God feel within themselves by the Holy Ghost from heaven, in the heavenly man, the sickle having cut off all earthy roots, all connection with the old creation. This presents and brings in a new seed, a heavenly people, a new creation, by the last Adam, the second man, the life-giving spirit. Short of this the elect seed mourn. The first sheaf has been waved and all the harvest is in it. The Holy Ghost is assured to all the seed, and so is the glory. One can count on it. This is the position from which Ruth and Naomi began to reckon by faith. Everything that followed happened in consequence of 'numbering from such time as thou beginnest to put the sickle to the corn.'

What occurs from this point onwards in the book of Ruth is truly wonderful. But it is also typical for all the children of God, taught of him to come to Christ 'in the beginning of barley harvest'. It is, I say, truly wonderful to observe the lovingkindness of the LORD, to see the end of the LORD in his ways with his people from the far country, to behold the grace of God in those who have endured the chastening of the LORD in all their afflictions and in all their tribulation. This is that suffering people, a people brought inwardly into peace and rest by the fulness of the Holy Ghost now, and who shall come out of great tribulation to worship the Lamb, and the Lord God Almighty, in the resurrection from the dead, in the inheritance of the world to come, in the coming day of glory. 'If ye endure chastening, God dealeth with you as sons.' How clearly this is set forth in the experience, example and type of Naomi and Ruth, even as in suffering and bitterness, lowliness and brokenness of heart, they appear in the heritage of the LORD 'at the beginning of barley harvest'. Amen.

IV

Hearest thou not, my Daughter?

BOOK OF RUTH 2:8, *Go not to glean in another field, neither go from hence, but abide here fast by my maidens.*

IT is necessary to grasp the work of God that had come to pass in Ruth and Naomi, and the spiritual place which they had reached, indicated by the last verse of Ruth chapter one. This presumes a tremendous change wrought in the two women. Spiritually they had come from the ministry of condemnation under Moses, to the ministry of justification in Christ; they had come from the gloom and darkness of mount Sinai, beyond Moab, to mount Zion, the perfection of beauty, out of which God shone. By faith, figuratively, their feet stood within the gates of the heavenly Jerusalem, and in the light of this the second chapter of the book of Ruth opens.

In contrast with these things, today there is a great deal of appropriating promises, texts and scriptures on the part of empty professors of religion, when the truth is that none has any right to the least text unless God himself impresses it within. He gave the promises, and he will surely make them good to all those to whom he applies them, and none other, let men 'claim' what they will. The salvation of God is his own prerogative. Even among men no man is justified in 'appropriating' what is in the gift of another. Lawfully the benefit must be bestowed by the benefactor. In Ruth, however, all is of God: one sees two women who are inwardly and deeply wrought upon by the Spirit and providence of God, women that have reached the place in their spiritual experience where their faith must and shall receive God's greatest and richest promises.

The book follows through the great work which God wrought upon their souls, so much of which appeared to them to be nothing but judgment, cursing and rejection, especially in the case of Naomi. No doubt over the past ten years she thought that there was no more religion in her than there was in the worst sinner in Moab. Doubtless, over all this terrible affliction, to her God was so far off, and the Almighty so bitter against her, that she felt herself for ever cast away, as if she could never find grace in his sight. And yet all this time he was watching her as the apple of his eye.

All the time this affliction, this sore distress, this taste of death, was God's work; but her sensations were such that she felt it could not be his work, unless it were to condemn her for ever. She felt the hiding of his countenance, the heavens as brass, an impenetrable barrier between an offended God and an accursed sinner. O, how dreadful she felt, how her soul was bowed down and crushed within her. How she felt, that of all people upon the face of the earth, she was the most out-cast and reprobate. And yet the very contrary was the truth: the very contrary. Ruth intuitively perceived this, but Naomi did not, and could not, for she knew by experience that the hand of the LORD had gone out against her, and the Almighty had dealt very bitterly with her.

Nevertheless, she heard a call when the word came to her that 'the LORD had visited his people in giving them bread', and she knew the voice that sounded, being enabled to say by grace 'The LORD hath brought me home', even if it were empty-handed, save for this Moabitess. So they came back 'In the beginning of barley harvest', that is, after the pass-over, indicating that the secret interior calling of the LORD had brought them into the good of a finished sacrifice divinely wrought and applied. They came into the place where expiatory blood had been shed. They came into the inheritance where bread had been freely given of God. And thus it was that they were fed.

Naomi and Ruth came in at the time at which the wave sheaf had been lifted up from the earth in the arms of ordained priesthood, whence Israel was counting the days, day by day, and the weeks, sabbath by sabbath, until the next great feast, the next event marking out the pilgrimage of God's people upon the earth. All Israel counted from the time when, on the morrow after the sabbath, the severed sheaf, the firstfruits, had been waved. They were reckoning a week of sabbaths, forty-nine days, knowing that on the fiftieth day the feast of Pentecost would come to fulfilment. They reckoned from the one to the other, and into such a reckoning of faith Naomi and Ruth were brought by the hand of the LORD, and the power of the Almighty.

If so, by faith they reckoned themselves to be in the worth of all that which God had purposed for his covenant people under the types and shadows of the Messiah in the old covenant. They reckoned themselves to be in the good of that which signified Christ crucified, dead, buried, risen, ascended, severed from the earth, and heir of the world to come. They reckoned to have a place in the man who rose from the dead, and an inheritance among them which are sanctified by faith that is in him. Thus they were seen in the counsels of God as having been crucified in the Lamb slain from the foundation of the world, as buried with him: sin, death, the curse, yes, and the law itself removed from the sight of God in the grave. They were seen as severed from this present world, as being in a new man, a risen man, a man of righteousness, of life, the quickening spirit, the life-giving Son, the second man, the last Adam, the heavenly man of glorious destiny.

Could all this—could so great people—be hidden in one small barley sheaf? Yes, seeing that God could multiply that which appeared so small to feed a great multitude, which no man could number, into thousands of thousands, and ten thousand times ten thousand, because of the worth, the value, the divine efficacy of the seed of God. By faith, seeing afar off, dimly perceiving in figure, type and prophecy, Naomi and Ruth were counting on this, reckoning from it. That was their position. That was the position of faith, and of the faithful, as the book of Ruth opens at the beginning of chapter two.

Ruth and Naomi believed. Their faith, wrought of God, reckoned from the place, the spiritual place, into which God had brought them 'in the beginning of barley harvest'. Therefore chapter two of the book finds them upon an altogether different plane, under a different dispensation, from that of the first chapter, the chapter of their affliction. Everything changes in chapter two, one finds an entirely new form of dealing. One finds that God is ordering their steps in a new and different way. That is the thing that I wish to impress: as a result of this appropriation of faith, of the reckoning of faith, into which the Spirit of God himself had led and quickened them, everything with Naomi and Ruth is different. It is striking: let us see how true this is.

The change does not come from Ruth and Naomi: they did not alter their own circumstances, and they could not alter their providences. Everything came from God. Having brought them from the land of their affliction, from under the work of the law, to the land of their inheritance, into the work of grace, the Spirit and providence of God unfold the wonderful destiny of those in whom his seed has taken root. Just observe how the chapter opens. They have returned; they have returned to the finished passover sacrifice; they have returned to Christ risen and ascended in a figure; they have returned to the work of faith with power; they have come into the good of the waving of the sheaf, and of God feeding his people. Truly in all this they can hear the words, 'For the LORD hath called thee as a woman forsaken and grieved in spirit, and a wife of youth, when thou wast refused, saith thy God.' 'For a small moment have I forsaken thee; but with great mercies will I gather thee.' 'In a little wrath I hid my face from thee for a moment; but with everlasting kindness will I have mercy upon thee, saith the LORD thy redeemer.' This is what we are about to observe, as we enter into the second chapter of the book of Ruth.

'And Naomi had a kinsman of her husband's.' Actually, in the Hebrew it is not 'kinsman'. The word is *moda*, meaning, 'a friend or acquaintance'. The word for kinsman, *gaal*, is not yet used. Namoi had a *moda*, a 'friend' or 'acquaintance' of her husband's, he was a mighty man of wealth, of the family of Elimelech, and his name was Boaz, Ruth 2:1.

If one were not so familiar with scripture many things might profitably be questioned which are otherwise accepted blindly. For example, here, the questioner might well ask 'What has that got to do with it?' What I mean is this: The sequence of events does not introduce this man Boaz in Ch. 2:1. He does not appear in the narrative of events, because he has not yet appeared on the scene. So far, there are just these two women, and, following on from the first chapter, one of them is about to say to the other—the daughter-in-law to her mother-in-law—'Let me now go to the field, and glean', Ruth 2:2. Then why mention this Boaz in Ruth 2:1? The man has not been introduced to them, he has done nothing which, in terms of the consecutive narrative, warrants his being mentioned at this point. He had not come into the lives of the two women, he has not yet entered the story, he is not part of what is taking place; still, he is introduced in the first verse, he is introduced now, that is, before he actually appears later. But why?

I want you to see that it is the Spirit of God who introduces Boaz in verse one, not the sequence of events then taking place. The sequence of events does not bring in Boaz until verse four, when, for the first time, coming out from Bethlehem to the field, he appears on the scene of action. Hence, I say, Boaz is not introduced by the sequence of events, which is focussed on the lives of Naomi and Ruth, because, at the time at which his name is first mentioned, he has had no contact with either of the two women, neither had he any place in what was then taking place. He was at that time not existent to them. But he was existent to the Spirit and providence of God.

Naomi and Ruth, however, were reckoning, they were counting, they were believing. Ruth says 'Let me now go and glean', and she does go and glean, but Boaz is not at all in the picture. In verse one he is brought to the attention of the reader before Ruth was aware of his existence. The Spirit of God introduces the man. I say again, the sequence of events does not introduce Boaz: the Spirit announces him before that time, and the Spirit explains that he is a *moda*, an acquaintance, of the family of Elimelech. Ruth does not meet this man in verse one, the verse in which he is announced. In terms of the record, the story, Boaz does nothing that he should be introduced in verse one. But the Spirit—as I may so speak— puts his finger on the man, and, inserting verse one into the sequence of events, says to the reader, as it were, Reader, I want you to mark this man, so that you may observe the wonderful ways of God.

That is the point: Boaz does not come into things yet, he does not enter the situation of Naomi and Ruth here, he is not at all in their view; but he exists, unbeknown, in the background, out of sight, and the reader is to notice his name now, and keep an eye on the man. There is a certain sense in which this man is brought in in connection with the passover, with the waving of the sheaf, with bread in the land, with reckoning until the day of Pentecost be fully come. He comes in in connection with the seed of Christ, he is of the promised seed, he is the promised seed for the time then present, and he is introduced—not to them, but by the Spirit of God—as soon as they, the two women, are brought to break bread in the promised land.

As soon as Naomi and Ruth are brought into the ways of God in his inheritance, as soon as they are brought into the knowledge of God in Christ by faith, God introduces this man. Not to Ruth. Not to Naomi. But to the reader. As if to say, There are these people brought to faith by the work of God, they are waiting upon him in submission, knowing not where to fasten their believing eyes, and I am showing you a man now, so that you can see what happens when they see him, and so that you can determine the issue of that faith which is of the real, solid and godly sort.

When the man Boaz actually comes into the narrative as such, Naomi and Ruth are going to recognise the hand of God, they are going to fall down before the LORD and worship, and say, This is the work of God. They are going to say, This man is of God and we are to fasten the eye of faith upon him. So the Spirit brings him in beforehand, that you should know this. How often has the Spirit of God said things, in our experience, prior to the appearance of the reason for the saying, and it has been marked by the watchers. That is what you have here. The Spirit shows us beforehand what he has prepared, and whom he has prepared, for those that wait upon him.

Thus the Spirit of God is saying to the reader, Reader here is a man that I want you to see; not coming into the narrative, but inserted—as a kind of parenthesis—into the narrative, nothing to do with the sequence of events actually taking place. The Spirit shows us whom he has prepared before that person enters the sequence of the story. The Spirit has prepared this man to meet everything that Ruth or Naomi could possibly desire, and, further, to fulfil everything for which they could possibly hope. The Spirit as it were secretly introduces the man to us beforehand to show us whom he has prepared in advance for faith, as if to say, Now watch, watch how this man, and the believing women, who do not know each other, and have not yet met, come together in the following narrative of events.

What the Spirit of God prepares is always embodied. It is always a man. Never a committee of men, never a bare idea or concept, however right. Truth must be embodied. It is all very well to talk of the word of God this, and the word of God that, and distributing 'portions' of scripture, or new testaments, but God says, 'How shall they hear without a preacher?' Not, How shall they read without the dead letter. The Ethiopian eunuch knew better and with more humility than these self-styled Gideons. The word of God must be embodied, and God himself must do the work within. Otherwise, it is man with the dead letter attempting to do the work of God in Arminian self-will.

It is all very well, and it was all very well, for people to read the words 'justification' or 'justified by faith', but until Luther received that shaft of light from heaven, until the words thundered into his soul as he ascended the Scala Sancta upon his knees—'The just shall live by faith'—to him as to others the words were mere speculative dogma. But when God brought his word into that man, his chosen vessel, everything changed. God inwrought his word in the man. It is always a man. Never a group, never disembodied. You say, That man is Christ. Yes, Christ and his seed. It must be embodied. You can take it, or you can leave it, but there it is, and it is true.

Of course, there must always be reference to the external rule of the word of God, that is not in question, the point is that when God works, he works by a man of his own choice whom he has prepared and in whom his word is embodied, a man who 'takes the book' and 'eats it up', who can say 'and it was in my mouth sweet as honey: and as soon as I had eaten it, my belly was bitter.' No doubt, under that anointing, others will be inspired; following on, great shall be the company of the publishers. But nothing can alter this principle. Really, there is no such thing as 'church' history. History is men, and 'church' history is men, and nothing else. Listen to the role: Abel, Enoch, Noah, Abraham, Isaac,

Jacob, Jephthae, Gideon, Samson, Barak, Samuel, David, Isaiah, Jeremiah, Ezekiel, Daniel, Ezra, Nehemiah, Hosea, Joel, Amos, Obadiah, and so on. Men whom God chose, whom God prepared, whom God sent, whom God anointed, and in whom God embodied the word of faith which we preach.

Observe how God laid hold upon John the baptist, even from his mother's womb. Consider the Acts: Acts of the Holy Spirit? Acts of the Scriptures? No, Acts of the Apostles, and, particularly, the apostles Peter and Paul, John being reserved for a later day. History itself, and certainly 'church' history, in the discernment of it, consists of perceiving the men raised up of God's providence. It is a man predestined. A man for the hour. The word of God in man. Even the gates and the foundations of the holy city, new Jerusalem, embody this truth, stretching endlessly into the world to come, the gates named according to the patriarchs, and the foundations designated after the twelve apostles of the Lamb. 'And Naomi had a 'kinsman' of her husband's, a mighty man of wealth, of the family of Elimelech, and his name was Boaz.' This is God's man for that time. Mark him, saith the Spirit. Can you hear this? Can you sense the direction of the Spirit in these words? It can be felt, as his voice can be heard. It is the truth.

Now then the Spirit records certain things about this man Boaz. It is not kinsman, *gaal*, it is *moda*, acquaintance; the subtlety being lost by the somewhat brutal handling of the translators. The Spirit does not bring in the intimacy of the relationship, or of its obligations, until realisation dawns later on in the minds of the saints. 'And Naomi had an acquaintance, a friend, of her husband's.' He was a mighty man of wealth: quite beyond the realm of her poor circumstances: how should such a man take notice of her? Yet he was of the family—however remotely connected—of Elimelech. There is this subtlety in the way in which the matter comes in, you see. Nothing obvious, nothing forward, observe. Just a suggestion, just a faint hint. And yet possibilities are there. Faintly, just faintly, the Spirit is hinting of that which is laid up in store.

The man Boaz had been on a friendly basis with her deceased husband, but more, there was some kind of relationship, some distant connection, he was of the family of Elimelech. So that things may pass from mere acquaintance, to a flesh and blood connection, a line may be traced, there is a relationship of family. And he is powerful. He is a mighty man of wealth. He can employ, he can sustain, and he can protect. Moreover he has the power to purchase. Now these are the essential qualifications of a *gaal*, a 'kinsman-redeemer', but nothing is said of this; the word, the key word, is not used. Here, almost in an off hand way, the man is introduced as possessing certain characteristics.

Redemption is exactly the need of Naomi and Ruth. It is in fact their only hope. But redemption presupposes an interested redeemer. Naomi once had land in Israel, but when it yielded no longer and failed to sustain life in famine, she went down with Elimelech and their two sons to Moab. The inheritance was lost in Israel. When the elder son died, the debtor's right passed to the younger son. When he died, the mortgage stood in Naomi, the wife of the dead, and the widows of the two dead men. But how could she redeem such a mortgage, who was reduced to the charity gleaning of a Moabitess in order to keep body and soul together?

The land had been theirs, but now it was passed out of possession by debt and by death. Yet there was a law in Israel, not a law of works, nor of a covenant of works, but a statute of grace, which was introduced by the gospel before preached unto them. There was a law in Israel that the nearest qualified relative who had power to do so, and was willing to do so, might buy back or redeem for the debtor the mortgaged land from whoever had bought it or had taken it over. Moreover the person who had taken it over, by law, had to sell. This was a statute in Israel.

Clearly the widowed paupers returning to the land could not buy, but if there should appear a *gaal* kinsman, provided he was the nearest kinsman established by law, and provided he was willing to part with sufficient money for the redemption from the present owner—who was obliged to sell—then the inheritance might return to the impoverished family. There was however, a further, hidden, legal problem, into which I cannot now enter particularly, but which will appear in the providence of God as the book unfolds to show the blessing of the Lord upon the believing people who reckon by faith 'from the beginning of barley harvest'.

Now it is clear that Boaz has been introduced by the Spirit—not the narrative—in Chapter 2:1. He is a friend or acquaintance; yes, but, however remotely, the family line can be traced: there is a matter of flesh and blood. Moreover he has wealth: great wealth, he is a 'mighty man of wealth'. He has the money, he is related: but is he willing? And even more important, in law, is he the nearest kinsman? We are told little at this point, save for these few brief hints. Ability is there, but it is a question of whether God will bring his ability to meet their poverty, it is a question of application.

In verse two of chapter two there is a short conversation between Ruth and Naomi. Notice that Ruth did not know, she had no idea, of the name of the owner of the field. She had said, Let me now go to the field, and glean. Naomi had replied, Go. And Ruth went, and came, and gleaned, and her hap was—mark that, her hap was—to light on the portion of the field that belonged unto Boaz. Boaz! The very man whom the Spirit of God had introduced beforehand. How easy it is to miss: the very man whom the Spirit of God had introduced.

However Ruth knew nothing of this secret of the LORD, revealed to the reader. Ruth had not the book bearing her name in her hand, looking for the field of this man called Boaz, of whom in fact she knew nothing. She did not know the owner of the field; had she known, the name would have meant nothing to her; she would not have known that any remote relationship existed; she knew nothing. Nevertheless the perceptive reader will follow the providence of God in the unfolding of his ways. For Ruth, without knowledge, the eye of faith was fastened upon the LORD God of Israel, under whose wings she had come to trust.

But whatever Ruth did not know, she reckoned by faith 'from the beginning of barley harvest'. That was what she believed, and she continued in the way of faith. She reckoned from that. Moreover she knew that she bore the solid fruits of such reckoning, and of a prior work of God in her soul. Her faith was seen by her works. Hers was no mere theory, or passive quietism. It was an active faith, one that could say in love, 'Entreat me not to leave thee, or to return from following after thee: for whither thou goest, I will go; and where thou lodgest, I will lodge: thy people shall be my people, and thy God my God: where thou diest, will I die, and there will I be buried: the LORD do so to me, and more also, if aught but death part thee and me.'

Ruth showed her faith by her works in Ch. 2:2, 'Let me now go to the field, and glean.' She wanted to work. She wanted to work, not for herself, but to support her mother-in-law. She had devoted her whole life to her mother-in-law. She is going out to work, to get her hands roughened in the fields, to provide a subsistence for her mother-in-law, to care for her in the house all the days of her life. That is rather different from the contemporary trend, is it not?

Observe Ruth's work of faith in Ch. 2:14, 'And she sat beside the reapers: and he reached her parched corn, and she did

67

eat, and was sufficed, and left.' You say, What work is here? Verse eighteen, 'And she took it up, and went into the city: and her mother-in-law saw what she had gleaned: and she brought forth, and gave to her that she had reserved after she was sufficed.' Ruth brought forth the whole ephah which she had gleaned, and gave it to her mother-in-law; but as well as the ephah, she gave also that which she had reserved after she was sufficed. It meant that, in verse fourteen, when Boaz reached her parched corn, she ate only part of it, reserving a portion to take back to her mother-in-law. 'She did eat, and was sufficed, and left.' She had no more than was sufficient to assuage her hunger, because she was saving for her mother-in-law. Hence she took back and gave not only the ephah which she had gleaned, but that which she had reserved from her own meal after she was sufficed.

That is the work of faith. It is faith which works by love. It is patient continuance in well doing, seeking for glory and honour and immortality, with the people and under the work of God. Just as was her entreaty in Ch. 1:16,17. She kept her vows; of course: because they sprang from that faith which works by love, which is the consequence of the quickening of the Spirit of God. You see this consistency in the twenty-third verse. 'She kept fast by the maidens of Boaz to glean unto the end of barley harvest and of wheat harvest; and dwelt with her mother-in-law.' She is keeping her promise, she is keeping her vows. It is no laborious work: she loves this woman; she has seen all that she wants in this woman. Love is the spring.

Once more the virtue of that faith, saving faith, the faith of God's elect, the faith which works by love, appears in Ch. 3:10,11 'Blessed be thou of the LORD, my daughter: for thou hast showed more kindness in the latter end than at the beginning, inasmuch as thou followedst not young men, whether poor or rich.' Shown kindness? More kindness? How rare this is: 'Charity suffereth long, and is kind.' But not much of the true nature of this quality appears with the relig- ious, especially with 'evangelicals', in my long experience. A show of it, a short burst of outward appearance, yes, for man to see, and self-esteem to relish, but inward love, no; interior abiding kindness, no. No, because love is of God, not man. Kindness is heavenly, not earthly. Only consider Ruth's kindness, wherein it consisted, and observe carefully the judgment of Boaz in the Spirit.

And again, Boaz says to Ruth, 'All the city of my people doth know that thou art a virtuous woman.' How was this? Because she stayed at home with her mother-in-law, going out for nothing but to work for their bread, keeping herself fast by the maidens—mark that, by the maidens—with modestly downcast eyes and true shamefacedness of spirit. Hearken to the apostolic rule: 'Let the young women be keepers at home.' It still applies. It applied here. It applies to appearance, even the length of hair, to the covering of the head at worship, in private as well, yes, and at the giving of thanks for meat, it applies to dress and clothing, it applies to the whole woman, commencing with 'the hidden man of the heart', radiating through the entire conversation. Godliness can never change. It respects the Eternal.

In the beginning, Ruth had no idea of the owner of the field in which 'her hap was' to glean, nor, had she heard his name, would it have conveyed anything to her. Much less would she have expected such an exalted personage to notice a mere gleaner, a Moabitess at that, taking advantage of the statute of charity in Israel. However, she did know that she reckoned from the beginning of barley harvest, and of the waving of the first-ripe sheaf on the morrow after the sabbath. She also knew that she had been brought by the LORD God of Israel under that blessing of Abraham which he had whilst yet being uncircumcised, 'Blessed be thou of the LORD, my daughter'. She knew that her faith bore fruit, this was plain and clear from her love to Naomi, a mother in Israel. She also knew that the Spirit of the LORD, who had wrought within her, attended that divine providence commanded to the heirs of promise in all their steps. And soon she was to learn what lay hidden behind such apparently casual events as 'her hap was to light on a part of the field belonging unto Boaz.'

At that time she had no idea of the command of heaven dictating her unwitting pathway, or the preparation of the LORD upon the heirs of faith. She had no hint, not the least idea, not the remotest sense of what would come, or that any-thing would come, of so natural a step. So necessary a step, to provide subsistence for her mother-in-law and for herself. That is the way God leads his people. She could at that very moment have been bleak with despair. She could have bent to pick out the corn with the tears blurring her vision, shaking her head that her eyes might clear before, rising, the women on either side might notice. She could have said within herself, I am destitute, a widow, alone. But 'her hap was to light on a part of the field belonging unto Boaz.' That is how it goes with the godly. But not with the light, frivolous, chaffy ungodly, who turn aside from the way of truth because they cannot wait, they cannot trust, God has kept them waiting too long, and they 'force themselves'. God has made the way of faith too long for false faith, for the presumptuous. So they go out. But providence cannot be hurried. God deals in time. And the saints bow in submission.

And, behold, Boaz came from Bethlehem, and said unto the reapers, The LORD be with you. And they answered him, The LORD bless thee. Notice the greeting. Here was a great man, a man worthy of respect. He spoke first. The fact that he was a man of humility and meekness was not the occasion of disrespect in the greeting of his inferiors. They greeted him as a superior. All this has gone in today's levelling world, the fallen church has followed suit: the effect is, the quality has gone. Here there is a recognition of relative station, of relative quality, of superior position. And notice the greeting: not 'Good morning', not comment on the weather, but—and he spoke first, as was seemly—'The LORD be with you.' And they

answered, 'The LORD bless thee.' How seemly: how spiritual.
This is how to greet one another, not in the forms of the
world, but, being transformed by the renewing of our minds,
according to the unchangeable word of God. Let the world,
and the hypocrites in the false churches, laugh away. He that
doeth the will of God abideth for ever: it is the world and the
fashion of it that pass away, not the abiding word of God. Let
your conversation be spiritual. Always and wholly spiritual.
Mark these things in passing, and the LORD be with you.

In verses five and six, chapter two, where Boaz addresses
his 'servant', the word should not be rendered 'servant' but
'young man'. There is a difference. When Boaz says, verse five,
'Whose damsel is this?' the young man answers, 'It is the
Moabitish damsel that came back with Naomi out of the
country of Moab: and she said, I pray you, let me glean and
gather after the reapers among the sheaves: so she came, and
hath continued even from the morning until now.' As the
two men observed Ruth, and as it became evident that she
was the subject of their conversation, how her heart must
have sunk, wondering if the great man would frown upon
this foreigner gleaning in his field after his own reapers.

But there is a law in Israel which declares that the poor are
to be permitted to glean behind the reapers. And it is law that
the owner and the reapers do not rebuke the poor that glean
after the sheaves have been cut and bound. The owner that
fails in compassion to the poor breaks that law. It is the law of
the poor, and a woe is upon him who is guilty of breaking it.
Nevertheless the young woman, Ruth, did not presume upon
right, she did not presumptuously commence gleaning, as if
she had rights, for she had spoken with humility and respect,
imploring the permission of the young man over the reapers.
'I pray you, let me glean.' It is all noticed.

Now for the first time Boaz and Ruth are face to face. He
calls her, and says, 'Hearest thou not, my daughter? Go not

71

to glean in another field, neither go from hence, but abide here fast by my maidens', Ruth 2:8. How overcome she must have been, that he should address her at all, and do so with kindness. But how much more overwhelmed that he should address her as 'My daughter'! That gave her an origin in Israel, who of herself and by nature sprang from Moab. She had renounced her origins in Moab, and had left both father and mother, and he says to her, 'My daughter', giving her parentage, giving her a place, giving her roots among the people of God.

He is so kind to her. Not only does he permit her to glean, but he offers her drink whilst labouring in the field. The tenth verse shows her response. She falls upon her face. It is hard for people to imagine one doing that today in the West, though I have seen this more than once in those overwhelmed by the grace of God in the East. As for me, where else should I be but on my face? She fell on her face, she bowed down to the ground, she said to him, 'Why have I found grace in thine eyes, that thou shouldest take knowledge of me, seeing I am a stranger?'

Her meekness, her submission, her lowly view of herself, her humility, all combine to give lustre and worth to her character. When Boaz addresses her, she is filled with wonder. She falls upon her face, that such a person as he should observe her, should talk to her. But that he should call her Daughter, overcomes her, she is overwhelmed by his kindness. Oh, why should he do so? She cannot understand that she, she should be shown such grace, such consideration, and that from one so exalted in station. It is beyond her understanding. That is always the way with the saints. That is the mark of those in whom saving faith is wrought: it is both inevitable and invariable. It is the deeply ploughed ground of heart-broken humility, that in which the seed has been sown and from which living faith shall and must spring forth.

72

Hearest thou not, my Daughter?

Why should Boaz show her such kindness? Why? He himself provides the answer: 'It hath fully been showed me, all that thou hast done unto thy mother-in-law since the death of thine husband: and how thou hast left thy father and thy mother, and the land of thy nativity, and art come unto a people which thou knewest not heretofore', Ruth 2:11. That was why she found grace in his sight. But when was all this 'fully shown' to Boaz? When? None of this was recorded as having been shown to him in the narrative. Nor was it said when the young man replied to Boaz in the field 'It is the Moabitish damsel that came back with Naomi out of the country of Moab.' Boaz' speech to Ruth, Ch. 2:11, reveals far, far more knowledge of Ruth than that conveyed by the answer of the young man. Boaz knew all her history. He knew about the ten years in Moab, and all that happened then. And yet there had been no contact with Naomi, the only other person who was aware of these things. But he knew.

How remarkable is this knowledge of Boaz. Who 'fully showed' such things to him? He knew her history, that was why he took notice. She was amazed; she was overwhelmed. Why? It had been fully showed him, all that took place ten years back; when her husband died; what she had done for Naomi; her address to Naomi when Orpah went back; her devotion to Naomi up to that very moment: fully showed him. Why did he show grace? That was why. He knows all her heart, all her works, all her life, and he says, before whose eyes all appeared as an open book, 'The LORD recompense thy work, and a full reward be given thee of the LORD God of Israel, under whose wings thou art come to trust', Ruth 2:12.

'Come to trust'; that is, come to faith. And saving faith, for it is the faith that works by love: the LORD recompense 'thy work', that is, the work of faith. That is what the LORD says to his people, 'I know thy works'. But Ruth never thought of cherishing Naomi, or the issue of her love for Naomi, as works. She wanted to do such things. But the LORD says, 'thy

73

works'. It was faith that worked by love, brought forth from a good and willing heart. She was unaware of it, never thought of it in that way; she might have said, 'When saw I thee an hungred?' or, 'When saw I thee naked, or in prison?' Inasmuch as she saw it in Naomi. She knew it not, but Boaz knew: he knew her history before she knew of his existence.

He knew all her history. He knew her before she knew him. That was what the woman of Samaria learned of a greater than Boaz, though of his seed: 'Come see a man that told me all things that ever I did.' That brought forth the saying, as she testified in wonder, 'He told me all that ever I did.' So it was with Nathanael. 'Before that Philip called thee, when thou wast under the fig tree, I saw thee.' This caused him—an Israelite indeed—to cry in worship before one with seven eyes, saying, 'Rabbi, thou art the Son of God; thou art the king of Israel.' Once more; this brought Zacchaeus down from the sycomore tree. What did? That he knew his name. How did he know his name? He had never been that way before, had never had the least acquaintance with Zacchaeus, how then could he look up and say, 'Zacchaeus'? How? Because he knows his sheep by name from everlasting. Because all things have 'been fully showed him' of his God and Father. For 'My Father worketh hitherto', and I work. Thus the Spirit of Christ wrought in Boaz, the seed of Abraham, the great grandfather of David, that he could say, 'It hath fully been showed me, all that thou hast done.' Hence Boaz made provision for her in abundance, Ruth 2:14-17.

The record of this eventful day, which commences at the second verse of chapter two, concludes with the conversation between Ruth and Naomi during the same evening, verses eighteen to twenty-two. Naomi observes that the amount brought back from the field—a whole ephah—vastly exceeded what could be expected from a day's gleaning. Nevertheless Ruth gives all to her mother-in-law, and not only so, but gives also that which she had reserved after she was sufficed from her own meal. What a comfort this must have been to Naomi, to see the evidence of such love, such kind thoughtfulness. When Naomi learns of the source of such bounty exceeding all expectation, then her comforts abound, and the consolation of Israel reaches her heart: 'The man's name with whom I wrought today is Boaz', Ruth 2:19.

Immediately Naomi perceived the hand of God. It is as if an awed hush fell upon the two women: the recognition that the Almighty, the LORD God of Israel, had brought together persons and circumstances ordained from ancient times. Here it was no longer 'her hap was to light upon'; this was the finger of God beyond all question of 'hap'. Said Ruth, His name is Boaz. And Naomi answered her daughter-in-law, 'Blessed be he of the LORD, who hath not left off his kindness to the living and to the dead.' And Naomi said, 'The man is near of kin unto us, one of our next kinsmen.' This was the first time that Ruth knew that he was related. Now, therefore, the possibilities open, as the counsel of God in blessing begins to unfold before her eyes. As to Naomi, she perceives immediately. She discerns the way in which the matter is going. She uses the word *gaal*—that is, kinsman redeemer—for the first time in the book of Ruth.

The awareness that the hand of God had brought into the life of Ruth—and therefore of herself—one next of kin, a *gaal* redeemer, does not excite Naomi into that kind of scheming and manoeuvring common to the flesh, much less does it launch her into presumptuous action. She sits still, waiting upon the LORD, watching for his hand. This is the mark of those who fear God, with whom is the secret of the LORD. Patience in waiting is the handmaid of faith, and Naomi quietly waits, as saith David, 'In waiting I waited for the LORD'. And so she counsels the younger woman, her daughter-in-law, who sits quietly in the house, listening to and absorbing the spiritual wisdom of Naomi in meek subjection. 'The aged women likewise, that they be in behaviour as becometh holiness' that 'they may teach the young women.' And so it was 'unto the end of barley harvest, and of wheat harvest' that Ruth 'dwelt with her mother-in-law.'

'So she kept fast by the maidens of Boaz to glean unto the end of barley harvest and of wheat harvest; and dwelt with her mother-in-law', Ruth 2:23. This hints at abiding principles for the people of God to the end of the age—for the 'wheat harvest' is the end of the age in a figure—irrespective of those distinctive providences peculiar to them as individuals at any point in time or in their pilgrimage. Such principles are common to all the people of God: by them the saints are marked out. It is well known that 'the harvest is the end of the world'. Until then the children of the promise walk as strangers and pilgrims on the earth in the light of the wave sheaf, of the counting till 'the day of Pentecost be fully come', of abiding in the patient waiting for Christ at the last day, at the harvest of the end of the world. That is the day in which the wheat shall be gathered into Christ's garner, but the tares shall be burnt with fire unquenchable, for the chaff shall be consumed with the stubble in the day of the LORD's wrath. Meantime, from the 'beginning of barley harvest' until 'the end of wheat harvest' the saints abide in meek submission, in the due order, according to the disposition of the Spirit and the direction of the word of God.

Observe the order that obtains. There is Boaz over all, not in the field as such, at Bethlehem. There is the young man over the reapers, and the young men that draw water. There are the reapers, the maidens of Boaz. And there are those who glean, the poor and the strangers, among whom was found Ruth the Moabitess. Everything, and everyone, had a recognised place and relationship under Boaz, according to the measure and order of life. It is not simply a question of being rightly related to Boaz—who after all was not in the field save at his own will—it is a matter of being rightly related to those above, beneath, and on either side of one. Again, not only was

Ruth's submission and meekness seen in the field, but equally her proper relationship at home with Naomi was transparent in its simplicity and contented godliness.

Both in the field and at the house Ruth was content with the lowly place granted her in grace and by the favour of the LORD God of Israel. She showed godliness and she showed submission, she showed contentment and she showed obedience. And she did so as the consistent rule of her life 'until the end of the barley harvest and of the wheat harvest.' Irrespective of any distinct or particular providences that might attend her, this was the rule that marked her conversation. This shows the true child. This is the order of God. This is what is exemplified for all the people of God, irrespective of the dispensation, in principle, by the words 'So she kept fast by the maidens of Boaz to glean unto the end of barley harvest and of wheat harvest; and dwelt with her mother-in-law'.

The summary and application is this: The saints are to continue from the barley harvest to the wheat harvest in the order and relationship of the house of God which obtained when the counting began, and which was established at the beginning. That is what is said, Acts 2:42, 'And they continued stedfastly in the apostles' doctrine and fellowship, and in breaking of bread, and in prayers.' There is order too: 'And fear came upon every soul:' that is towards God; 'and many wonders and signs were done by the apostles': not by anybody else, which is the death-knell to pentecostal and charismatic pretensions, which are out of the order of God, for they know nothing of his house, neither of his power nor his authority. There is a right relationship, an historic as well as a continuing fellowship. The apostles, the apostolic signs, and the apostolic age were unique, but the ministry is not: the 'young men' continue. 'But continue thou in the things which thou hast learned and been assured of, knowing of whom thou hast learned them', II Tim. 3:14, commanding continuation after the apostles' departure.

'Take heed unto thyself, and unto the doctrine'—the apostles' doctrine—'continue in them', I Tim. 4:16. The 'young men' are to continue. 'That thou mayest know how thou oughtest to behave thyself in the house of God, which is the church of the living God, the pillar and ground of the truth'. 'That thou mayest know', the epistles were written, and subjection was required. All must be in its due place, 'from the barley harvest unto the wheat harvest.' This is true even down to the 'gleaners'. 'For I say'—that is, the apostle says—'to every man that is among you'—that is, among the saints—'not to think of himself more highly than he ought to think; but to think soberly, according as God has dealt to every man the measure of faith.' Then from a broken and contrite spirit that trembleth at his word, everyone, each in his own place, must be 'perfectly joined together, having the same mind and the same judgment'. Bound together in unity, subject to the apostles' doctrine and fellowship, breaking of bread and prayers, everyone will assuredly 'speak the same thing'.

How this exemplary spirit, seen in Ruth, is reflected in the church, that is, the gathering of the saints by one Spirit under the headship of Christ, until the end. 'Let your women keep silence in the churches: for it is not permitted unto them to speak; but they are commanded to be under obedience, as also saith the law.' What is it to us that the world—followed by the apostate church, and splintered sects—has thrown everything over? Ruth in her conversation teaches us to abide in Christ; teaches us to submit to those raised up of God over us for the care of the house of God; teaches us to be subject to those at home and in the field; teaches us to watch even until the coming of the Lord. Therefore we should continue stedfastly in the apostles' doctrine and fellowship, and in breaking of bread and in prayers, so that it may be with us as with them at the beginning that 'fear came upon every soul.'

There is no thought in the mind of God of condoning division, denominationalism, sectarianism, or independency.

There is one fellowship, in any given place, and in every place together. Most may depart, and in this day probably have departed, but the LORD abides faithful, and is even now bringing back the exiles from Moab. 'And they continued stedfastly in the apostles' doctrine and fellowship', coming together in one Spirit into that of which it is written, 'that ye may have fellowship with us: and truly our fellowship is with the Father, and with his Son.' Fellowship, the one fellowship, that is, fellowship that is unchanged to this day, the abiding fellowship, is in the Eternal. Worldly changes alter nothing. The apostasy cannot touch the everlasting. This is that union, that visible company, which is in God the Father and in our Lord Jesus Christ. Into this, after so long a time, he is again leading his people in the last days, so that we can bear testimony, though it be but by twos or threes. Where such are, there is he in the midst. This is that which was in the beginning, is now, and ever shall be. 'So she kept fast by the maidens of Boaz to glean unto the end of barley harvest and of wheat harvest; and dwelt with her mother-in-law', Ruth 2:23.

V

Seek I not Rest for thee?

BOOK OF RUTH 3:1, *My daughter, shall I not seek rest for thee, that it may be well with thee?*

THE book of Ruth moves from winter through spring to the summer, following the farming year of the people of the land. As it does so, the agricultural events, seedtime and harvest, drought and plenty, become spiritual illustrations and figures. Indeed, some of the figures, taken from the farming activity and husbandry of the children of Israel, had been incorporated by the law of Moses into the worship of God's people centuries before, thereafter to be enacted annually in connection with the keeping of the feasts.

Nevertheless these ritualistic forms were not intended to be viewed in an outward or legal way: they were 'figures of the true', types and shadows for the time then present of the gospel of Christ and of the kingdom to come. The book of Ruth itself opens with God's judgment upon the land, the drought and famine showing his severe displeasure and wrath upon his people. That was how his anger was made known to the people in the land: the famine was due to no natural cause, God's wrath was the cause. The narrative takes up the beginning of barley harvest, the waving of the first-ripe sheaf —all immensely significant of the coming work of God in Christ for his people—and follows through the counting of the fifty days until Pentecost, when the first harvest is brought home.

Whereas the barley harvest is recorded as having been gathered—a great golden heap in the midst of the threshing-floor—the book looks forward to and envisages the gathering of the wheat harvest at the close of the year. All this is of great prophetic importance. However the third chapter of the book of Ruth in particular points to a special time in this sequence of events. It is a chapter centred about the winnowing of the barley harvest, brought into the threshingfloor, and, as in every other case, these natural events are given a heavenly and spiritual meaning in Christ for those able to receive their true import. 'He that hath an ear, let him hear.'

The figurative use of the husbandry of the land ought not to surprise us. The Lord Jesus in his doctrine constantly used agricultural illustrations. 'I am the bread of life', he declared. In him the living saw life from the dead, and perceived how to separate the wheat from the chaff. The parable of the sower and the seed declared the progress of the gospel from the glory. The parable of the mustard seed showed the distorted growth of the work on the earth. The parable of the leaven manifested the working of sin within the heart of the meal prepared for the generation to come. The parable of the tares opened to the discriminating the work of the apostles, the sleeping of their successors, the hidden sowing of Satan, the duplication of every feature of the work of God, and the confusion reigning in the world in consequence.

The barley loaves in the feeding of the five thousand, Jesus being made known in the breaking of bread at Emmaus, the vineyard in the parable, the figure of the vine, all reveal invisible, interior and inward truth otherwise hard to be grasped. 'I am the true vine', said Jesus, 'and my Father is the husbandman.' 'I am the vine, ye are the branches.' 'If a man abide not in me, he is cast forth as a branch, and is withered.' Here is the work of Father, Son and Holy Ghost. Here is the election and the reprobation. Here every divine mystery is opened and made plain by the figure of the true.

The use of the loaf to signify 'This is my body', of the cup to show forth 'The new testament in my blood', illustrate from the fruit of the field what is divine, heavenly, and spiritual. 'The harvest is the end of the world', yes, but which harvest? And what is the barley harvest? The herds and flocks, the sheep and the goats, even the bulk of the camel, are all subservient to things invisible and unseen as yet, made to serve divine ends. We are told in Christ's doctrine, Except a corn of wheat fall into the ground and die, it abideth alone, but if it die, it bringeth forth much fruit. This fruit is that which is brought into his garner in the last day, whilst the tares shall be burnt with fire unquenchable.

These things being so it is hardly surprising to find the old testament full of such types, shadows, figures and illustrations of that which was to come in the new testament. Moses in the law made abundant use of the agricultural events in the yearly farming cycle in order to set forth Christ in the gospel. Nowhere is this utilisation of the husbandry of the people and land of Israel more wonderfully opened than in the book of Ruth. And nowhere more in the book of Ruth than in the third chapter. This is the chapter to which our attention is now being directed.

'Then Naomi her mother-in-law said unto her, My daughter, shall I not seek rest for thee, that it may be well with thee?' Ruth 3:1. Observe the word 'Then'. This indicates a specific point in time, prior to which certain conditions had obtained. For fifty days from 'the beginning of barley harvest', Ruth 1:22, until 'the end of barley harvest', Ruth 2:23, an unbroken and uniform period of activity had passed. More or less, between passover and Pentecost, conditions were unchanged. Ruth had 'kept fast by the maidens of Boaz to glean until the end of barley harvest.' Boaz had spoken graciously to her at the very beginning, but no more. Ruth had gone about her business with quiet industry, and now the work was concluded. Boaz was no longer to be seen in the field, and neither were the reapers. The fields which had held the standing corn, waving gold in the sunlight, animated by the figures of the workers,

were now empty. Nothing remained but stubble. The reaping
was over. The harvest was home.

'Then' Naomi her mother-in-law said unto her, 'My daughter,
shall I not seek rest for thee, that it may be well with thee?'
Although the two women had for some ten years passed under
the chastening yoke in Moab; although the Almighty had
brought them home again; although they had come into the
good of the slain lamb at the time of the passover; although
God had set before them the figure of Christ risen as the
wave sheaf on the first day of the week; although they counted
themselves by faith to be of that harvest secured in him;
although they had eaten of their own ephah from the lord of
the harvest: Naomi knew that this was not enough. She
knew that there must be a further approach to the man of
blessing, and that the further blessing could come from no
other. But she would not be presumptuous. She would wait
in the fear of God until God in providence without, and by
the Spirit within, testified to her spirit: 'Then.'

Naomi watched while the barley harvest was being gathered
in. Naomi waited throughout the fifty days, reckoning by
faith. 'Then' in her spiritual wisdom, she perceived by the
Spirit a change in the providence of God, commensurate with
the ending of the old and the beginning of the new phase of
husbandry. She had seen the hand of God in the harvest,
where others saw only the harvest. She perceived the work of
God in the winnowing, where others saw nothing but the
winnowing. Naomi's eyes were open, all the time she was
watching and waiting upon the LORD God of Israel. 'Then', at
the end of the harvest, and at the beginning of the winnowing,
she knew that God's time had come. Just as she discerned
that it was for Ruth, not her, to take the step of faith and
approach the man of blessing.

Certain features are conspicuous in Naomi at this time. For
example, her waiting in faith, during which time nothing

would induce her to move. Likewise her moving in faith when nothing would induce her to wait. The living character of her faith, alert to what was called for by changing circumstances, so that what was then right was now wrong, and what was then wrong was now right. A time to wait, and a time to move. Vital faith in the living God; watching a changing providence, and waiting for a witnessing Spirit: these things Naomi exemplified. Another conspicuous feature seen in Naomi at this time was her sure knowledge, despite all that she had received, that there remained much more to be possessed.

So it was that Naomi the mother-in-law of Ruth said unto her, 'My daughter, shall I not seek rest for thee?' Naomi discerned that no matter what they had been brought into—and they had been brought into very much—nothing was established or permanent without the obtaining of 'rest'. Their need was for their own inheritance with the people of God in the land of promise. Naomi's desire was for Ruth to have an abiding place of rest in Israel. A heritage peculiar to her. That is what Naomi meant by 'Shall I not seek rest for thee?' There could be no settlement short of this inheritance. Like the dove, Genesis 8:9, there was no rest—it is the same word—for the sole of her foot until the land of promise appeared. Says David 'He leadeth me beside the still'—again it is the same word—'waters': the waters of rest. It was for the shepherd's leading to such an inheritance that Naomi sought. She knew that there remained a rest for the people of God; she knew that it was entered into by faith; and she knew the man towards whom faith was to be exercised if ever rest was to be obtained.

But transcending all this, just as her faith soared past Boaz through distant David to the great redeemer to come, Naomi's faith rose above the fields of Bethlehem-judah, beyond the borders of Israel, to the land that was very far off, the heavenly country. 'My daughter, shall I not seek rest for thee?' There remaineth therefore a rest for the people of God, and none but one greater than Boaz could bring into it. 'Shall I not seek rest for thee?' They that say such things declare plainly that they seek a country. And, truly, if they had been mindful of that country from whence they came out, they might have had opportunity to have returned. But now they desire a better country, that is, an heavenly: wherefore God is not ashamed to be called their God: for he hath prepared for them a city, Heb. 11:16.

Although the rest immediately sought by Naomi for Ruth was the inheritance in Bethlehem-judah, and although the redeemer through whom she sought for it was Boaz, nevertheless because that land represented the heavenly country, and because Boaz signified the coming redeemer, therefore both the world to come and Christ himself were the real objects of Naomi's faith. This is true of all the heirs of faith. 'These all died in faith, not having received the promises, but having seen them afar off, and were persuaded of them, and embraced them, and confessed that they were strangers and pilgrims on the earth.'

Just as the heirs of promise under the old covenant regarded the heavenly inheritance of the world to come in terms of the figure of the land of Israel, and viewed the redeemer from sin and death, the seed of Abraham, as typified for the time then present by such as Boaz, so the saints of the new testament, without a cloud, past all types and shadows, look directly at the same heavenly country, and view immediately the same redeemer, Jesus Christ himself. Even more clearly than Ruth and Naomi, the people of God under the new covenant know that there can be no resting place this side of death, and no inheritance other than in the world to come. Hence the seeking rest, so conspicuous in Naomi in a figure, is not peculiar to her, but common to all the people of God under whatever covenant, not in the passing figures of the true, but in the abiding heavenly realities themselves.

It is precisely this being 'pilgrims and strangers on the earth', the looking for a better resurrection, the pressing towards the heavenly inheritance through the redemption that is in Christ Jesus, that distinguishes the saints from the world in all ages. This is what marks out the sojourners in Hebrews eleven. It is the most singular characteristic of the people of God, the unmistakable mark of the elect, it is that which enrages the empty profession of religion, and causes the world to swell with hatred. 'If ye were of the world, the world would love his own: but because ye are not of the world, but I have chosen you out of the world, therefore the world hateth you', Jn. 15:19. Here is the mark of the pilgrim in all generations: 'Hear my prayer, O LORD, and give ear unto my cry; hold not thy peace at my tears: for I am a stranger with thee, and a sojourner, as all my fathers were.'

In the book of Ruth, chapter three and verse one, the watching and waiting of Naomi came to an end. She knew that the time to move in faith had arrived. For all that she had gained, she was aware that the great issue of the inheritance remained unresolved. And she was equally aware that the LORD would indicate the time when the issue should be resolved. When the barley harvest was home, when the winnowing began, when Boaz went down to the threshingfloor, then she knew that the time had come. 'Then.' Then said Naomi unto her daughter-in-law, 'My daughter, shall I not seek rest for thee, that it may be well with thee?' Naomi had perceived that it was not for herself but for the young woman Ruth to take the step of faith. And, in her wisdom, she counselled her accordingly.

Naomi knew that Ruth's need was for a certain place, an abiding place, in Israel. Ruth's need was for a place with the people of God in the inheritance. She desired that Ruth should have her own heritage in the land. This Naomi called 'Rest'. That was what she meant when she said, 'Shall I not seek rest for thee?' Of course she referred to her lost heritage in the

fields of Bethlehem-judah. But through that earthly inheritance, through the figure, her desire for Ruth's abiding blessing
soared to the heavenly country, reached out and up to the
true, it pierced to the glory of the world to come. That is the
'rest' that remains for the people of God. And, ultimately, in
the Spirit, that is the rest Naomi most desired for Ruth. But,
under the law, in the figure, through the type, by the providence of God, this must be seen and set forth in the actual
acquisition of the earthly field of inheritance. Yet it transcends
this altogether. The godly woman rested in hope. This was
the hope that was set before them upon which the inward eye
of Naomi was fixed. It was hope that she had in mind.

What is hope? Peter, on the day of Pentecost leaves us in no
doubt as to the hope of the saints in past generations under
the old covenant, saying, Ye men of Israel, hear these words;
Jesus of Nazareth, a man approved of God among you by
miracles and wonders and signs, which God did by him in
the midst of you, as ye yourselves also know: him, being
delivered by the determinate counsel and foreknowledge of
God, ye have taken, and by wicked hands have crucified and
slain: whom God hath raised up, having loosed the pains of
death: because it was not possible that he should be holden of
it. For David speaketh concerning him, I foresaw the Lord
always before my face, for he is on my right hand, that I
should not be moved: therefore did my heart rejoice, and my
tongue was glad; moreover also my flesh shall rest in hope:
because thou wilt not leave my soul in hell, neither wilt thou
suffer thine Holy One to see corruption.

Mark those words 'Rest in hope'. According to Peter, David,
being a prophet, and knowing that God had sworn with an
oath to him that of the fruit of his loins, according to the
flesh, he would raise up Christ to sit on his throne; seeing
this before, spake of the resurrection of Christ: that his soul
was not left in hell, neither his flesh did see corruption. This
is to rest in hope. It is the hope of the resurrection. If so, then

the 'rest' sought by Naomi for Ruth might have been typified by but it could not be confined to the inheritance of a field in Israel. There is no 'rest' that death will not irrevocably disturb: then, 'resting in hope' pertains to the resurrection. There can be no earthly inheritance that the last judgment will not dissolve: then, 'resting in hope' refers to the heavenly inheritance of the world to come. By the figure—and through it—Naomi meant the true, the hope of Israel, unto which the twelve tribes, instantly serving God, hope to come. But hope that is seen is not hope. For what a man seeth, why doth he yet hope for? Then Naomi viewed the land that is very far off.

Likewise Paul the apostle, an Hebrew of the Hebrews, testified before the council of Israel, 'I am a Pharisee, the son of a Pharisee: Of the hope and resurrection of the dead I am called in question', Acts 23:6. And if the council of Israel, if an Hebrew of the Hebrews, if two generations of Pharisees understood by the 'rest that remains to the people of God', the hope and resurrection of the dead, speaking thus for all the old covenant people, how could Naomi have meant anything else, when she said 'My daughter, shall I not seek rest for thee?' So confirms Paul of all the children of Israel, saying, 'So worship I the God of my fathers, believing all things which are written in the law and in the prophets: and have hope toward God, which they themselves also allow, that there shall be a resurrection of the dead, both of the just and unjust', Acts 24:14,15. And of the just, from ancient times, none was more conspicuous than Naomi seeking the rest that lay beyond the grave, not for herself alone, but for the believing Gentile also, even that rest that stands in the hope of the resurrection and the inheritance of the world to come.

Indeed, this seeking a better resurrection, a better country —though both were typified in Israel in this present world— marked all the children of Abraham. For father Abraham himself 'Against hope believed in hope', Rom. 4:18. Against hope? What hope? Any hope of anything from this life, or any hope of inheriting anything in this life. Believed in hope? What hope? The hope of the resurrection from the dead, and the hope of the inheritance of the world to come. To Abraham, the effect of death, and of the dissolution of the creation, could not touch the hope. Why not? Because his hope was in resurrection, and in a new creation. And why should it be thought a thing incredible that his true daughter Naomi, born hundreds of years after his decease, should share the same aspirations, the same faith, and the same hope as the father of the faithful?

This hope, that of the glory of God, shall never make us ashamed, in whose hearts the love of God is shed abroad by the Holy Ghost. For the same Holy Ghost is the earnest of our inheritance, till the redemption of the purchased possession. This purchased possession will be seen in the resurrection of the body, and that inheritance, in the glorious world to come. This is the 'rest that remains to the people of God', and, by the Spirit, to it God's people are sealed. Even the creation groaneth and travaileth under the bondage of corruption, seeking rest, which shall not come till the manifestation of the sons of God in glorious resurrection liberty when time shall be no more. Till then the creation is subjected in hope. Then so is the land of Israel with each several inheritance. Then Naomi's seeking rest was not in the earthly inheritance, but through it, to everlasting glory.

Because of the certainty of this resurrection in the seed of Abraham, and of that inheritance in the seed of David, we, with all saints, rejoice in hope. There is joy in hope. Because it is established, it is the blessed hope. It is settled in Christ raised from the dead, secure to all the seed: for the Lord God shall give unto him the throne of his father David, and he shall reign over the house of Jacob for ever, and of his kingdom there shall be no end. How can there be an end when it is the hope of eternal life, and when it pertains to an everlasting kingdom? Here is sure and certain rest, precisely that sought by Naomi for Ruth. Seeing then that we have such hope, we use great plainness of speech. Now the glory of God is revealed in the face of Jesus Christ, and the God of glory, the God of hope, hath secured the promise to all the seed, whereof he hath given assurance by the resurrection of Jesus Christ from the dead, sealing the title to the heavenly inheritance by the Holy Ghost to every heir of promise.

Hope is the expression of that yearning which because of the inward work and illumination of the Holy Ghost, views and longs for the resurrection and the world to come. It is that which inspired Naomi to say to Ruth 'My daughter, shall I not seek rest for thee?' And it is that which inspired Paul to pray for the saints at Ephesus, that they might know the hope of his calling, and the riches of the glory of God's inheritance in the saints, Eph. 1:18. One might have supposed that when Paul heard of faith in the Lord Jesus, and love to all the saints, on the part of the brethren at Ephesus, he would have said 'I cease not to give thanks for you, making mention of you in my praise.' Not so. He says, 'I cease not to give thanks for you, making mention of you in my prayers.' What, interceding for them, after such faith, such love? But what of such hope? This lack urges Paul to cry for a spirit of wisdom and revelation in the knowledge of Christ, for not otherwise would they perceive what is the hope of God's calling, or what the riches of the glory of his inheritance in the saints.

This is similar to Naomi. She had come so far: faith in Christ in the passover, in the wave sheaf, in the spiritual meal, yes, and in Boaz himself, even to the end of barley harvest. Yes, but what of the inheritance, what of the redemption, what of the 'rest that remains to the people of God?' 'Then Naomi, Ruth's mother-in-law, said unto her, My daughter, shall I not seek rest for thee, that it may be well with thee?' It is for a title and a witness to the rest, the inheritance, the redemption, that her spirit seeks, and so does Paul's: the one for Ruth, and the other for the saints at Ephesus. The same is evident in the Colossian epistle, where Paul, hearing of their faith in Christ Jesus, and of the love which they had to all the saints, far from resting satisfied—though he fails not to give thanks for that whereunto they have attained—prays always for their increase. But in what? In 'The hope that is laid up for you in heaven.' This hope must be illuminated to them, and must ever be kept in mind, seeing that it comes by nothing other than a spirit of wisdom and revelation in the knowledge of Christ, further to faith and love, and is called, 'the hope that is set before us'. This is what Naomi sought for Ruth.

The Colossians, once alienated and enemies in their minds by wicked works, were now reconciled in the body of his flesh through death, that God might present them holy and un-blameable and unreproveable in his sight, if—mark that, if—they continued in the faith grounded and settled, not being moved away from the hope of the gospel. Then their not being moved away from the hope of the gospel was that which would make their calling and election sure. This is evidently set forth in the church of the Thessalonians which was in God the Father, and in the Lord Jesus Christ, of whom Paul could say 'Knowing, brethren beloved, your election of God.' But how could he know this? Because his gospel came not unto them in word only, but also in power, and in the Holy Ghost, and in much assurance. And not only so, for their faith and love, so evident at the beginning of the work, found its confirmation in their patient continuance in the hope of the gospel, pressing forward to the rest that remains to the people of God, as he says, 'Remembering without ceasing your work of faith, and labour of love, and patience of hope in our Lord Jesus Christ, in the sight of God and our Father.'

Paul's seeking rest for the saints, and Naomi's seeking rest for Ruth, appear to coincide in spirit with these words: 'Looking for that blessed hope, and the glorious appearing of the great God and our saviour Jesus Christ.' If it should seem too much that Naomi could have been so perceptive, beyond the form of an earthly inheritance, and the type of a natural redeemer, let it be recalled that centuries before, Abraham, to whom the land was promised as an earthly inheritance, nevertheless 'desired a better country, that is, an heavenly'. As to the true redeemer, bringing redemption from sin and death, it is said of all the patriarchs, long before Naomi, 'These all died in faith.' But faith in whom save the redeemer Jesus Christ? Then why should it seem a thing incredible that Naomi should share like precious faith with those who preceded her by centuries, seeing that she, with them, died in faith 'Looking for that blessed hope, and the glorious appearing of the great God and our saviour Jesus Christ', whose coming should awake their sleeping dust. For to them and of them it was said, Thy dead men shall live, together with my dead body shall they arise. Awake and sing, ye that dwell in dust: for thy dew is as the dew of herbs, and the earth shall cast out the dead. Isa. 26:19.

It is quite true that when Naomi said to Ruth, Shall I not seek rest for thee? the rest to which she referred was that of an inheritance for the time then present in the land of Israel, and that the redeemer to whom she looked was Boaz. And yet it is easily shown from the epistle to the Hebrews that the believing saints, such as Naomi, looked for another rest entirely, and another redeemer altogether, notwithstanding the fact that under the old testament of necessity such faith must be exercised through—and not irrespective of—the earthly types and shadows. So that for them, even in the land, even though the inheritance had been redeemed, notwithstanding the fact that they rested in their present heritage in the land of Israel, yet the true rest of faith still 'remained', the hope was yet 'set before them'.

Those that believed under the old covenant did not consider themselves to have inherited the promises, but only the type of the promises, only the shadows. They looked for a city, they looked for a country, they looked for a redeemer, beyond all that was earthly, temporal, of this world, or of the present age. These all died in faith, not having received the promises, but having seen them afar off, and were persuaded of them, and embraced them, and confessed that they were strangers and pilgrims on the earth; for they that say such things declare plainly that they seek a country. And Naomi said such things. So did the old testament saints who were in their country, in that land promised to them, in possession of their inheritance. Then why did they say such things? why did they still look for a country? Why? Because they knew that this was not their rest. And so did Naomi. There remaineth therefore a rest to the people of God.

The epistle to the Hebrews assures us that the land of Israel was not the rest of the people of God—but only a figure of it— just as it declares plainly that the old covenant people of God who inherited that land still continued to look for an inheritance in glory and for a country that was heavenly. And this was true from the very beginning: then, if such things were spoken of Abraham, how much more are they true of Naomi hundreds of years later?

Likewise David—quoted in Hebrews 4:7—testifies, 'Today if ye will hear his voice'. Hear his voice saying what? Saying 'If they'—the children of Israel—'shall enter into my rest', verse five. Enter into rest 'Today'? But had they not entered into rest under Joshua, centuries before? How then could David say, Today? Enter into rest in David's day, after so long a time since Joshua had led the children of Israel into the promised land of rest? If Joshua had given them rest, why did David say in his day, some four hundred years later, 'Today, if ye will enter into rest'? Surely, if Joshua had given them rest, David would not afterwards have spoken of entering into another rest in his own day? This shows that the earthly inheritance of the land was not the promised rest, but was a figure of the promised rest.

'There remaineth therefore a rest to the people of God', Heb. 4:9. And Naomi, having inherited a parcel of ground in the rest provided by Joshua for the tribe of Judah, afterwards lost everything in the famine. Nevertheless she sought redemption for Ruth. In reality, however the faith of Naomi looked through the things which could be seen to the things which could not be seen, at the things which were invisible. The eye of her faith pierced beyond the rest of the inheritance of a parcel of ground in Bethlehem-judah, to the heavenly rest that remains for the people of God at the end of time. That is, she looked past death, beyond the grave, to the resurrection, at the glory of an everlasting inheritance, world without end, Amen.

VI

The Threshingfloor

BOOK OF RUTH 3:2, *Behold, he winnoweth barley tonight in the threshingfloor.*

THE first four verses of chapter three record the crucial counsel of Naomi to her daughter-in-law. Here is one of the great turning points in the book of Ruth. We have seen the motive for Naomi's counsel: 'My daughter, shall I not seek rest for thee, that it may be well with thee?' What follows is the advice Naomi proposes to Ruth concerning the means by which that rest is to be obtained. To it Ruth responds 'All that thou sayest unto me I will do.' This is the subject of the third chapter of the book of Ruth.

Naomi continues with the words, 'And now', verse two. Now. That is, a certain point in time had been reached. It was to the very day. In fact it was toward the end of that day when Naomi spoke the vital words 'He winnoweth barley tonight'. Tonight. Toward the close of the day, as the evening drew on, Naomi said, Now. It is a great thing to be able to watch in faith, week after week, day after day, hour after hour, finally to be enabled to conclude with certainty, to the very hour, 'Now'. There is a time to wait in faith: then to move would be sin. There is a time to move in faith: then to wait would be sin. It is a matter of spiritual discernment. Naomi had that discernment, and Ruth had the humility to follow it. Now.

Naomi had waited for some fifty days. This had commenced at the passover with the lifting up of the wave sheaf towards heaven in the arms of priesthood. She had numbered from the morrow after the sabbath; 'from the day that ye brought the sheaf of the wave offering; seven sabbaths shall be complete: Even unto the morrow after the seventh sabbath shall ye number fifty days.' Now the harvest was home. The day of Pentecost had fully come. The day had come when 'Ye shall bring out of your habitations two wave loaves of two tenth deals: they shall be of fine flour; they shall be baken with leaven; they are the firstfruits unto the LORD', Lev. 23:17. So that after some fifty days the vast mound of golden corn lay ready on the threshingfloor: Pentecost had come: the firstfruit loaves had been waved. And Naomi said, 'Now'.

Naomi herself did not move. Naomi did not leave the house. Naomi sat still, for she knew in her wisdom that it was Ruth who must move in faith, and so her counsel ran, and to it the younger woman was attentive and obedient. Naomi, in her perception and awareness, albeit keeping still in the house, knew exactly what was taking place. She knew in the Spirit what was taking place outside without leaving her place. And she knew whose faith was to be active when the time came indicated by the word 'Now'. She directs Ruth to Boaz himself. It was to be a great step, to move towards Boaz, who represents Christ in his present work in his people. It is movement toward Christ himself, in view of the fact that a certain point had been reached in time. Certain new conditions obtained. A point had been reached, there was achievement, and on the basis of that achievement Boaz—or rather Christ—is to be approached.

Naomi, in her counsel, directs Ruth in the way of faith. But she will only help the young woman so far: Ruth's faith itself must be perceptive as well as active. Although Naomi had said early on 'The man is near of kin unto us, one of our next kinsmen', Ruth 2:20, using the key word *gaal*, or 'kinsman-redeemer', she does not use this word now. She says, Ruth 3:2, 'Is not Boaz of our kindred', where the word is *modath*, a form of the expression *moda*—acquaintance, family friend, kin—

used in Ch. 2:1. Now, one may have a thousand *moda*, or *modath*, but not one redeemer. What Ruth and Naomi needed was redemption. They needed not a *moda*, but a *gaal*. And yet Naomi, in casting Ruth on the way of faith, although she had progressed from *moda* to *gaal* beforehand, reverts now to *modath*. Why? Because Ruth must perceive for herself, and act for herself. She must act in faith from her own perception. Counsel may come from Naomi, but wise counsel will see that the spring of action comes from the exercise of Ruth's own faith.

So there is encouragement for Ruth to move toward a family friend, one who has authority and power. She is to move towards him at a certain place, at the place of winnowing, in the threshingfloor, the place where the grain is separated from the chaff. She moves to one who can distinguish between the solid seed and the empty chaff. He can evaluate the worth. Now Ruth knew that there was that which was solid in herself, answering to the weighty seed, there was an inward work wrought of God, and she knew that Boaz was the man of discernment who could estimate this aright. She was also well aware that there was chaff about her too. She was aware that she had chaff, but then, so had the corn in the threshingfloor. She knew that she could safely bring everything to him, because he was a man who would judge righteous judgment. He was a man who could discern the grain from the chaff. And that was what she wanted, first of all, in and for herself. That is the point that is 'now' reached in experience.

'Behold, he winnoweth barley tonight in the threshingfloor': here is the occasion of Naomi's counsel. Winnowing is that work of the harvester that follows on from flailing. A flail is a wooden staff at the end of which a short heavy stick hangs swinging. It is a hand threshing instrument. The heap of barley is first flailed, that is, it is threshed: the harvesters move in to the golden heap of grain, hardly seen for the clouds of dust, arms rising and falling, the flails flashing up and down, as they flail the whole harvest of barley, beating, threshing, until not a grain remains but that it has been beaten with the flail. Why is this? It is to beat off the chaff. The lord of the harvest cannot abide chaff, and, in consequence, the whole harvest must be flailed, it must be threshed, for by no other means can the chaff be separated from the grains of barley to which it clings.

Only after this stage comes the work of winnowing. Although the chaff has been beaten off the grain, it is all loose mixture, and the lord of the harvest will not have loose mixture, he will have pure grain. Therefore the next step for the harvesters is to separate the grain from the loose chaff lying among the pure seed. The process by which this is achieved is called winnowing, and that is the work with which Boaz was occupied that very night. 'Behold, he winnoweth barley tonight in the threshingfloor.' Winnowing is the work by which the grain is freed from mixture with the chaff. The heap of barley—grain and chaff together—is tossed up into the air, shovelled high, so that it cascades down in a golden arc onto the threshingfloor. But as this takes place, as the barley is thrown up, reaching its apex, to drop again, so the winnower vibrates the great fan in his hand, creating a strong draught which blows directly through the stream of barley whilst it is being cast up into the air, and during the time that it takes to fall down. The effect of this is to blast away the chaff, which is of course light, whilst allowing the weightier grain to fall down into its place by itself. In the end therefore, there exists a pile of pure golden grain, a golden hill, by itself in one place, and, driven into the sides of the threshingfloor, a great pile of chaff wholly separated from the pure seed.

How many view Christ in such a way? As fulfilling this activity in the church? But it is all precisely figurative of his work with his people from the beginning of time to the end thereof. Then it is what he is doing still with his people, in the fulfilment of it, at this present moment: 'Now'. It is not the wheat harvest: that is the end of the world. It is the barley harvest: this came in on the day of Pentecost. Winnowing therefore signifies the present work of Christ in his true people. Then where are they? To whom does this occur in the Spirit? To every one of Christ's people, and to none other. If so, it is evident, professing Christendom, and particularly evangelicalism, and 'evangelistic' activity, is full of pretence, because the process of flailing, fanning, winnowing, and separating the chaff from the pure seed is what never happens to them, in the heavenly equivalent of it. It never takes place in such circles. Never. Where they are, is where the chaff is.

Chaff characterises that which is of the flesh; it is that light, outward, airy, flippant part, the fleshly part, the part which the Lord cannot away with. Here it is not the flesh as brought to light under the law. It is the flesh as brought to light under the gospel. It is the chaff clinging to the pure seed, and clinging so tightly that nothing can loosen it, save the flail. The flesh takes occasion of the work of God to assert itself. The gospel becomes the means of self-assertion. Christianity today is absolutely full of such chaff, and empty of grain: the churches are full of it, evangelism is full of it, yet the Lord never deals with it, neither has he part nor lot in their matters. They are none of his. Nevertheless our Boaz, in our day, 'Winnoweth barley tonight in the threshingfloor'. That is how you may tell who are his.

He is winnowing. He commands the flailing of his own, disregarding all other. This work marks them out, and, for all the chaffy mouthing of scriptures, all the light talk of Christ, all the empty vain profession of youthful keenness, all the frivolous, fleshly efforts in evangelism, those to whom this never happens are none of his. His flail falls only upon his own. 'For whom the Lord loveth he chasteneth, and scourgeth every son whom he receiveth. If ye endure chastening, God dealeth with you as with sons; for what son is he whom the father chasteneth not? But if ye be without chastisement,

99

whereof all are partakers, then ye are bastards, and not sons.'
Then they are not sons, they are the teeming children of the
bondwoman in religion.

Christ is still winnowing. By this his few true people may
be distinguished beyond any doubt. And by the lack of it the
bastards, the hosts of bondchildren—no matter the scripture
in their mouths, the claimed blessing in their lives—by the
lack of it, I say, the bastards and the bondchildren are brought
to light. Christ is winnowing still: he flails, scourges, separates;
he threshes and beats, to bring to light the flesh with its sin
and worldliness, clinging to the gospel, in the most subtle but
tenacious of all connections. His flail surely separates that
part which is of the flesh, namely, sin acting in relation to the
gospel seed, that which is light, empty, flippant, airy and
frivolous. The flail beats all of this off the children of promise,
and the chastening, scourging and beating ensures that the
seed of God's planting remains intact and separated to the
Holy Ghost in every true child of God.

The flesh is discerned in all its subtle working: not only the
flesh in its obvious manifestations, but the whole of the carnal
part as it works in a profession of Christ: in the meetings of
the saints; in the church; and clinging to the Spirit and word
of God in the ministry. The great thresher of heaven spares
not, he beats off all the chaff, and as a result of this long and
heavy flailing, the solid, inward, weighty part becomes distinguished from the light, carnal, outward show. The inward
and solid seed finds an answer in the saints. They walk in the
word of God, abiding in the Father and the Son, the seed
planted deep in their hearts, full of the life and power of the
Holy Ghost. All is separated from the working of the flesh in
the outward man by the mighty strokes of the flail, the winnowing of the thresher, by which scourging work the godly
are brought to light under the hand of God. The ungodly are
not so. All their religion is chaff, corresponding to the outward man, and what may be seen of men. Their gospel is in

the flesh. Their form of creed and religion is in tradition and the dead letter. They are like the chaff, which the wind driveth away.

The Lord from heaven winnows still: 'Whose fan is in his hand, and he will throughly purge his floor, and gather the wheat into the garner; but he will burn up the chaff with unquenchable fire.' That is, at the last day, for the wheat harvest is the end of the world. But the principle is equally applicable to the barley harvest, in which he purges his people, from the day of Pentecost even until the days of the poor scattered remnant at this present time, he continues his work. His mighty arm vibrates the fan, God's powerful providences lift up and cast down, the wind bloweth where it listeth, and the divine thresher knoweth whence it bloweth, for the heavenly wind of the Holy Ghost blasts through the soul of every one of his own people, separating chaff from grain, flesh from spirit. Thus he sanctifies his people unto himself, to walk and to dwell in the Spirit, made free from the working of the flesh, as from the airy and worldly superficiality characteristic of all the hypocrites in Zion.

This is the work that brings the people of God out from among them. Not the will of man in the dead letter, as it is this day with all the envious, evil-speaking, and jealous bastard Calvinists, pretenders to 'reform', who never had the root of the matter in them in all their lives, whose whole religion stands in the energy of the flesh and in the traditions of men. No; it is the flail and the fan in the hand of the heavenly man that separates the true seed of God, even in our own times, whilst God works a work in our day which they will in no wise believe, though a man tell it them. It is by the wind of the Holy Ghost, which they cannot command, which bloweth where it listeth, it is by these crushing providences, which they know not, by tearing afflictions, inward experiences, real vital union, by these things, I say, it is by these things that the true seed is revealed, as it was in the beginning, is now, and ever shall be, Amen.

Yes, but what have we today? We have self-styled, man-taught hireling pastors, the product of yesterday's pile of chaff, standing around the present untouched harvest, tongue-in-cheek, piously intoning 'We are not to judge, brother, Leave the chaff alone: Who do you think you are? you are not to judge!' That is exactly what is happening. But what they say, and do, judges the Lord of the harvest, not the true servants of the Lord of the harvest, who are of that harvest. But the truth is, the Lord judges them, and his words find them out. Found out, they then resort to the works of their master, namely, envy, lies and persecution against the true servants of the Lord, whom God chose instead of them.

'He winnoweth barley tonight in the threshingfloor.' If 'tonight', it is, spiritually, until the day dawn, and the shadows flee away, and, if so, it is indicative of the present age. As to the threshingfloor, this is the earthen floor where the flailing and the winnowing take place: it is upon earth. Here the word of the Lord tries his people. Here the seed of the word within his people must be divested of the chaff of the flesh, of the flesh working upon and through that word, divested, I say, by way of the flailing, threshing, winnowing, and separating. This is the work that is wrought in the earth upon the people of God by the Lord of the harvest from the heavenly glory, and by it they are made manifest.

In view of this, in the figure of the true, the shadow of the spiritual substance to come, Ruth is to wash and prepare herself, Ruth 3:3, she is to present herself in terms of what the LORD has done for her, for none come into the threshingfloor of the LORD save those that have title to the everlasting inheritance. All must show their birthright, they must prove their anointing, they must declare their regeneration, the garment of praise must be theirs, in a word, they must be true-born children. It is this that is indicated by Ruth's washing, anointing, and clothing herself, with the water, oil, and garments given of the Holy Ghost to the elect children. None other may enter into the threshingfloor, and none other shall come under the heavenly flail, the divine fan, or the spiritual winnowing of the Son of God.

Ruth is to wash herself, she is to come in the washing of regeneration, the laver of the Holy Ghost, because God saith, 'I will take you from among the heathen, and gather you out of all countries, and will bring you into your own land. Then will I sprinkle clean water upon you, and ye shall be clean: from all your filthiness, and from all your idols, will I cleanse you.' Ruth felt this, and thus presented herself. She was to anoint herself. By faith she knew that he who had established her with the people of God, and had anointed her, was God. She had received an unction from the Holy One of Israel, the anointing which she had received abode in her, and, whilst in subjection heeding the counsel of Naomi—who had been under the anointing before her—she needed not that any man should teach her. The same anointing taught her all things, and was truth, and was no lie, and even as it had taught her she was to abide by faith in the Messiah to come, set forth in the figure of Boaz.

Ruth is to present herself not only in terms significant of her quickening and of her anointing, but she is to put her raiment upon her. It is her raiment, for God himself had clothed her with the garment of salvation, he had covered her with the robe of righteousness, and these were her own possession and pertained to none other. These garments given unto her are the beautiful garments of the daughter of Jerusalem, as the daughter of a king, garments of wrought needlework, all glorious within, clothing of wrought gold. All is of God, and of this, arraying herself in her raiment is a figure, for God had given her beauty for ashes, the oil of joy for mourning, and the garment of praise for the spirit of heaviness. 'Wash thyself therefore, and anoint thee, and put thy garments upon thee', to present to the Lord of the harvest the work of his own hands, the operation of the Spirit of God, and the blessing of the Most High, that he might perfect that which concerned her.

Ruth is thus counselled by Naomi to get her down to the floor, but not to make herself known unto the man until he shall have done eating and drinking. Then, 'when he lieth down', she is advised to mark the place where he lies, and go, and uncover his feet, and lie down. As to the rest, saith Naomi, 'he will tell thee what thou shalt do.' Yes, and the Holy Ghost shall lead her, and faith shall know by that anointing what words to speak. This movement which Naomi advises Ruth to take by faith violates the best in worldly standards. It is a violation of ethical standards. And, judging by what I have experienced of lies, backbiting, evil speaking, rumour-mongering, false witnessing among 'Bible-believing Christians', and 'reformed' hypocrites, poor Ruth would fare ill if she were known by them to have taken such a course as laid her open to their evil surmisings. Woe be to Ruth if this had taken place in our present apostate evangelicalism, that is, in this generation of tittle-tattling thinkers of evil, 'pastors' and people alike, who far from 'thinking no evil', do nothing but think evil and construct it in every circumstance where they are able to do so especially against the true servants of God, of whom they are so envious. Nevertheless this is the course of faith counselled in the Spirit by Naomi, and the pure and chaste Ruth will answer to it in obedience, let men think or say what they will, and so it is with us to this day.

Before Ruth is advised to approach Boaz, he must have finished certain things: he must have finished flailing, threshing, winnowing, and separating the grain from the chaff. He must have finished eating and drinking. 'And it shall be, when he lieth down, that thou shalt mark the place.' This indicates a certain state in Boaz. He has rejoiced over the work that he has done, he has feasted with the labourers, his heart is merry, and he lies down at the extremity of the heap of corn, resting in the completion of the threshing and winnowing, taking in every single grain of barley, rejoicing in the harvest.

Boaz, according to the counsel of Naomi, will then be in a position of rest regarding the labour of the threshingfloor.

The grain has been brought in, it is in a golden heap before his eyes, and he is satisfied in respect of the purity of that seed. Here it is not a question of typifying the finished work of the cross. It is a question of typifying what was brought in—or harvested—by that finished work being divested of the chaff of the flesh in experience. Here, it has been divested. The Spirit of Christ in Boaz is able to rest in spiritual appreciation of his inheritance in the saints, seen as gathered on earth in a separate body for his own glory and satisfaction. To talk of 'the finished work, brother', and live in an undisciplined, unspiritual, worldly and carnal state, is sheer contradiction. To talk of the work of the cross whilst attending the outward form of services and meetings with a mixed multitude of converted and unconverted, worldly and spiritual, of the living and the dead, is nothing but disobedience. What is of God should come out and be brought into the threshingfloor, the place, and the only place, where the Lord will cause the grain to be separated from the chaff.

The figure of what the finished work of the cross will bring in for the Lord—in any given generation—is a finished heap of golden corn, separated from the chaff, and gathered by itself in unity. Thus he who can abide no chaff in the midst, resting and at peace, will rejoice in the work of his own hands. This signifies the people of God in deep self-judgment, broken in heart and contrite of spirit, constantly mortified, instantly penitent, melted, yielded, submissive, continually under self-abasement, kept humble and low, united in one company, spiritual and weighty, under the powerful operation of God's Spirit by the word of the truth of the gospel. Here is a people who can judge between the world and the church, the flesh and the Spirit, the law and the gospel, Christ and Moses, Sinai and Zion, this age and that which is to come, the bondchild and the freeborn, the hypocrite and the guileless. And not only judge, but keep out the vain, airy, flighty spirit, and keep in the inward weighty power of the

Holy Ghost. These keep the seed of the word of God safely within. This is that for which Christ looks. This is what manifests his finished work: all else is presumptuous talk. The finished work is manifested in and by the winnowed barley harvest, nothing else. If that finished work appears not in the barley harvest, why should it be supposed that it will appear in the wheat harvest? It is 'Now' that the Lord would rest in his work. This is indicated by the word 'Tonight'.

That night Ruth went down to the floor, and did all that her mother-in-law bade her. For when Boaz had eaten and drunk, and his heart was merry, he went to lie down at the end of the heap of corn. Boaz lay down at the extremity of the heap of corn, that is to say, he measured the yield of the harvest to its full extent, and rejoiced, resting in the worth of the entire flailed and winnowed yield. In the things of Christ, of which the winnowed barley harvest was the figure for the time then present, Boaz signified the Son of God, just as the harvest set forth his gathered people in whom the word had been sown, brought in by his powerful, separating, sanctifying work in any given generation. The Lord ought to be able to come to the company of his people today, and take his rest in the satisfaction of what he has harvested by his death, and what he has flailed and winnowed in his risen life, to be of his own pure seed alone. This is what he did under the ministry of the apostles in the beginning, and it is what he would do with his gathered people in any given age.

That was the purpose of his finished work on the cross, as it pertains to the testimony in this present age. That is, so that the people of God might be gathered together in one, in the Father and the Son, that the world might know that the Father sent the Son. Of this the heap of winnowed grain at night in the threshingfloor was a vivid and illuminating figure. This pure seed of God is the result of the work of the ministry, of the perfecting of the saints, of the edifying of the body of Christ, in its fulfilment by the Lord from heaven in the church below. With this purpose in Christ, the early apostolic ministers were in full sympathy: it was the aim and object of their ministry, 'that ye also may have fellowship with us'. This ministry has been lost in our day, being supplanted by a system that is clean contrary—opposite in principle—to what was in the beginning. The current false ministry of man's devising has no sympathy whatsoever with the aim, purpose and intention of the Lord of the harvest. There is neither sending nor communion nor communication.

The Lord of the harvest allows not one single flake of chaff to remain unjudged. The pure seed must be separated in each, and separated in all. This is most conspicuous when one considers the apostolic epistles of the new testament. Everything is brought under the flail of the Lord, the winnowing of the Son of God from heaven, the powerful operations of the Holy Ghost below. To this the apostolic ministry exactly corresponded, speaking experimentally and doctrinally in that divine operation which would mortify the flesh, beat out the chaff, separate the solid seed of the word of God, and keep the light, airy and carnal outward man judged and subdued by the mortifying and quickening work of Father, Son and Holy Ghost. How clearly this appears—in another figure—in the letters to the seven angels of the seven churches in the book of the Revelation: the Lord knows but one standard, to which the ministry must measure and answer: the seven golden candlesticks. By that standard everything must be judged in the church without compromise. There is nothing of this today, just as the true church is not gathered today, because in the present profession, there is nothing answering to the ministry of John. Indeed, there is no prophetic ministry apparent in current evangelicalism.

How different is the picture seen in Boaz! He is wholly at rest in the yield, he is resting at the outermost edge of the fruit of his labour, he is taking in with joy the whole of his work brought to fulness in the threshingfloor, as it pertained to the current year. That is to say, spiritually, in that contemporary period. Boaz signifies Christ resting in the completeness of his sanctifying work from heaven brought to light during any given generation. All the yield is there. He has compassed the whole of the harvest which he has gained for the Father out of that particular age—or, in the figure, that year—and he reposes with satisfaction in the attitude of rest. Boaz is tranquil, contented, his repose signifying Christ at rest in a people gathered as one in all the good of his justifying and sanctifying work on their behalf. They are set apart from the world and rotten religion, from the chaffy, light profession of the dead letter. They are united together as one body. This is his rest for ever: here will he dwell; for he hath desired it. And so Boaz teaches the people of God in a figure.

Ruth came softly, and uncovered his feet, and laid her down. Uncovered his feet? Why was that? why did Naomi advise her to do this? It was because she knew that, as the cold of the night drew on, the resultant exposure would awaken him naturally. Ruth knew the presumption of accosting him; throughout the past fifty days she would not draw attention to herself, she waited until such time as Naomi in her wisdom directed. When the time came, she did not presume to rouse Boaz directly, but, even as Naomi counselled, she ensured that he would wake of his own accord. She dare not awaken him. She waits, and she acts with discretion. Said Naomi, Uncover his feet, and lay thee down; and Ruth did so, assured that he would awaken in due course without further intervention. To Boaz, awakening would have seemed entirely natural, because what Ruth had done hours earlier would have been unknown to him. Thus in meekness and self-effacement, but determination and courage, Ruth moves in faith towards her redeemer.

'And it came to pass at midnight, that the man was afraid, and turned himself: and, behold, a woman lay at his feet. And he said, Who art thou? And she answered, I am Ruth, thine handmaid: spread therefore thy skirt over thine hand-maid; for thou art a near kinsman', Ruth 3:8,9. Ruth waited through the long hours. And it came to pass at midnight, at the darkest hour, that the man stirred: he was afraid. He was conscious that things were out of place. Something was wrong. He became aware of a strangeness: 'And it came to pass at midnight, that the man was afraid, and turned himself.' Someone was there, it was a woman in the threshingfloor, and Boaz called out, 'Who art thou?'

Observe Ruth's reply. Naomi had given her no guidance. She had said, 'He will tell thee what thou shalt do', verse four. Naomi had not advised Ruth what to do, on the con-trary, she had said the man would tell her what to do. But, at midnight, far from telling Ruth what to do, he cried out, 'Who art thou?' Thus Naomi shut up Ruth to faith, to being cast upon the LORD, to being dependent on the Spirit, and, in the moment of Boaz' awakening, Ruth was confronted with this point-blank challenge, upon the right answer to which so much depended. But her own faith, that which had been wrought of God in her, that weighty, divine, and living seed, inspired her utterance, giving her words to speak equal to the occasion: 'I am Ruth, thine handmaid, spread therefore thy skirt over thine handmaid, for thou art a near kinsman.'

This was the word of faith, just as it was the utterance of the Spirit. There was nothing of the flesh here: the chaff had been beaten off, and driven away. It was all the manifestation of the seed of God. In the flesh Ruth might have justified herself, saying, 'Do not misunderstand, there is absolutely no impropriety in my being here, there is nothing wrong with my intention as a woman at midnight at the feet of a man in the threshingfloor.' How easily she could have been misunder-stood, how inevitably nature would expostulate, crying out the innocency of its intention. But there is none of that. No chaff, no flesh. Ruth's answer was of the Holy Ghost, not of self-justification. She appeals to him, but does not protect herself.

Her answer was spontaneous, she did not rehearse these words. How could she? She did not know what he would say when he awoke, however much she turned it over and over in her mind during the long dark hours of waiting. Ruth lifted her heart to God and put her trust in him, so that in the issue she answered meekly and submissively, yet so strongly and spiritually, thus showing the guileless honesty of her heart. Moreover, by this she revealed how highly she esteemed the understanding of Boaz, and the uprightness of his judgment, valueing the grace of this great man at whose feet she rested her cause.

She answered, I am Ruth, thine handmaid. She sets herself in relation to him by these words; not, I am Ruth, but, I am Ruth thine handmaid. Thine handmaid. It is a relationship to which she appeals, yet it is a relationship of the lowliest possible order. She appeals from the place of self-abasement and humility. A mere handmaid, yes, but 'thy' handmaid. It is thine, thine. This relationship is less than he had said to her in chapter two, verse eight. There he called her 'my daughter'. But meek and lowly, she will not presume, she 'claims' nothing, she does not rise so high, no, it is 'thine handmaid'. How many would so speak? Even as many as the Lord our God shall call.

Because she is Boaz' handmaid, she waits upon his initiative. She looks to him alone. 'Behold, as the eyes of servants look unto the hands of their masters, and as the eyes of a maiden unto the hand of her mistress; so our eyes wait upon the LORD our God, until that he have mercy upon us', Psalm 123:2. She has been watching his hand these fifty—or more—days past. She has no other resource, she will appeal to none other. Consider her submission, her obedience, her meekness. Such circumspection in her reply at such a time, and in such a place. Yet this was indeed the right place: the place where the chaff had been detected, beaten off, cast out. The place where the pure seed was discerned, valued, and stored up. Of this she was well aware, and appealed to him with a calm pure faith, presenting to his judgment the worth of all that heavenly seed which the LORD had planted and through which he had wrought in her heart.

'Spread therefore thy skirt over thine handmaid.' This is a figurative expression, but it is evocative of much to Boaz. It speaks of all that Boaz could give, and everything that Ruth could desire. The word 'skirt'—spread therefore thy skirt—is *kanaph*, a word that has been translated 'skirt' some fourteen times. Yes, but seventy times more—fourteen multiplied five times over—the same word has been translated 'wings'. *Kanaph* is in fact the word, the same word, used by Boaz to Ruth in chapter two verse twelve, 'The LORD recompense thy work, and a full reward be given thee of the LORD God of Israel, under whose wings thou art come to trust.' Now Ruth quotes the word used by Boaz, who had spoken to her of her trust under the *kanaph* of the LORD God of Israel. Ruth, I say, uses the same word to Boaz, saying, 'Spread therefore thy *kanaph* over thine handmaid.' How evocative, how appealing, indeed, how challenging to Boaz.

But what and where are the wings of the LORD God of Israel? David, the offspring of Ruth, informs us in the Psalms that he rejoiced in the shadow of his wings—though at that time he was in dire straits in the wilderness of Judah—and the reason that he rejoiced beneath his wings was explicit: hitherto God had been his helper. Indeed, his language in adversity was constant, saying, Psalm 57:1, In the shadow of thy wings will I make my refuge, until these calamities be overpast. And in another place David declares that the excellency of God's lovingkindness is the moving cause because of which men shall put their trust under the shadow of his wings.

As to the place in which the wings of the LORD God of Israel are found, where else should this be but in his own house, and in the sanctuary of his own presence? Where but above the very mercy seat itself? This is set forth in a figure in the holy of holies: 'And the cherubims spread out their wings on high, and covered with their wings over the mercy seat, with their faces one to another; even to the mercy seatward were the faces of the cherubims', Ex. 37:9. Once more, 'The cherubims spread forth their two wings over the place of the ark, and the cherubims covered the ark and the staves thereof above', I Kings 8:7. Of course, the figure is of the cherubim; yet the reality is of the LORD God of Israel. It is this of which Asaph speaks when he prays 'Thou that dwellest between the cherubims, shine forth', Psalm 80:1. Between the cherubims, yes, but beneath the shadow of their wings, from above upon the mercy seat, God spake to the children of Israel, and there his presence was made known. This was the place where the blood of atonement was sprinkled, it was the propitiatory, the place of reconciliation, it was at the heart of the sanctuary, and of the covenant. He who enters with boldness into the Holiest of all by the blood of Jesus, by that new and living way, which he hath consecrated for us, through the rent veil, that is to say, his flesh, is most surely in the secret, and shall certainly be covered with his feathers, trusting beneath his wings, Psalm 91:4.

This experience is to have the wings, or skirts, spread over one indeed, and must be preceded by a work of God under the law, or, figuratively, by ten years in Moab, during which the filthy fountain of the flesh, and the iniquity of one's sin, are brought wholly to light, whilst an inward and spiritual discovery is made of the wrath and indignation of the Almighty. 'For thus saith the Lord GOD unto Jerusalem: Thy birth and thy nativity is of the land of Canaan; thy father was an Amorite, and thy mother an Hittite. And as for thy nativity, in the day thou wast born thy navel was not cut, neither wast thou washed in water to supple thee; thou wast not salted at all, nor swaddled at all. None eye pitied thee, to do any of these unto thee, to have compassion upon; but thou wast cast out in the open field, to the loathing of thy person, in the day that thou wast born.'

'And when I passed by thee, and saw thee polluted in thine own blood, I said unto thee when thou wast in thy blood, Live; yea, I said unto thee when thou wast in thy blood, Live. Now when I passed by thee, and looked upon thee, behold, thy time was the time of love; and I spread my skirt over thee, and covered thy nakedness: yea, I sware unto thee, and entered into a covenant with thee, saith the Lord GOD, and thou becamest mine. Then washed I thee with water; yea, I throughly washed away thy blood from thee, and I anointed thee with oil. I clothed thee also, and girded thee about with fine linen.' Now, this was the experience of Ruth, who had come to trust under the wings of the LORD God of Israel. For, lo, she came to the man of his right hand and said, 'Spread now thy skirt over thine handmaid.' That is, take me under thy headship, bring me beneath the anointing that goeth down even to the skirts of the garments, make me as bone of thy bone, and flesh of thy flesh. 'Spread therefore thy skirt over thine handmaid; for thou art a near kinsman.'

And now Ruth herself uses the expression *gaal*, kinsman-redeemer. Naomi had referred to a *moda*, or family acquaintance, at the first, Ruth 2:1. Days later she told her daughter-in-law that he was far more than a *moda*, he was a *gaal*, a kinsman-redeemer, Ruth 2:20. However, when the time of winnowing had come to pass, and Naomi would counsel Ruth, she avoids the deeper, the more significant word, and reverts to *modath*, Ruth 3:2, casting Ruth upon her own experimental faith in the issue. And in the issue, the Spirit by whom Ruth had been taught, gave her the very words to speak, the utterance of faith to reach to the heart of Boaz, and set the work of redemption in motion: 'Thou art a *gaal*.'

From now on the book of Ruth is focussed upon redemption. Ruth had come out with the real ground upon which she sought Boaz. This appears in the use of the word *gaal*, uttered by Ruth for the first time, but evidently long pondered and esteemed by her faith. Before Boaz, what she believed in her

113

heart she confessed with her lips. Henceforward the relationship shifts dramatically from 'handmaid' to 'near-kinsman'. The attention is now focussed upon redemption. Boaz understood immediately that Ruth had Naomi's welfare at heart in her outwardly bold and daring act of faith: but had she the right? She was a Moabitess, it was true, but then she had married the son of Elimelech and Naomi. The legal right existed. But, whatever the right, it was for love of Naomi that she had done this. Boaz sees that. Naomi was the connection. In Moab Naomi had lost her inheritance. She had lost her title in Israel, it had all gone, she had lost her heritage. And it was for her, her welfare, her inheritance, that Ruth jeopardised both reputation, honour, and all else, in seeking the favour of Boaz. Boaz perceived this immediately.

It was not for her own sake that Ruth was in the threshingfloor that night: it was for Naomi's sake. It was for the redemption of Naomi's inheritance that she made this daring and touching appeal. Yet it was also true that if Naomi was the object of her love, the spring of her actions, she herself was fully involved. 'Thine handmaid': for 'thou art a *gaal*.' The appeal is focussed upon Boaz being a redeemer to Naomi, but that appeal widens greatly and significantly to include the redemption of Ruth. Redemption applies to three things: the person; the house; and the land. It is not only a matter of the redemption of the person from insolvency. It is a matter of redeeming the whole house. Ruth is involved with Naomi. 'Thou shalt be saved, and thy house.' There is also the question of the inheritance, the redemption of the purchased possession, the heritage of the people of God. All come under the scrutiny and competence of the 'near kinsman', the *gaal*.

In his reply, Ruth 3:10-13, first Boaz assures her that he understands fully her motive and intention in approaching him in the threshingfloor. He does not do this directly, but indirectly, by expressing his appreciation of her worth: 'Blessed be thou of the LORD, my daughter: for thou hast showed

114

more kindness in the latter end than at the beginning, inasmuch as thou followedst not young men, whether poor or rich', Ruth 3:10. He declares his esteem of her character: 'Thou hast shown more kindness in the latter end.' Kindness to whom? To Boaz? Had she shown more kindness to Boaz? Certainly not. He is expressing appreciation of her work. What work? The work of her kindness. If it be enquired, To whom? I answer, not to Boaz, for Ruth had given nothing to Boaz. Her kindness was to Naomi.

Boaz knew that Ruth had shown such kindness to Naomi. He shows his valuation of this, and sets it in relation to the work of God: 'Blessed be thou of the LORD.' He perceives that this is of God, this love of Ruth for the saints; he realises that this woman's care, her giving up all prospects—'Thou followedst not young men'—was from the LORD. It is for her kindness to Naomi that he expresses such appreciation, discerning it as the work of God in Ruth. The remarkable truth that emerges here is the way in which Boaz knew everything about Ruth's past, and her care for Naomi over the time past; though Ruth thought he knew nothing at all. Moreover Boaz perceived all that lay behind the kindness of Ruth, seeing it in the light of the whole testimony of her life, as being 'blessed of the LORD'.

'Thou hast showed more kindness at the latter end than at the beginning.' Latter end of what? Beginning of what? At the latter end of the harvest. What she had done now, in taking her honour and life into her hands and coming down at night into the threshingfloor, all for Naomi's sake, showed even more kindness than that shown by the young Moabitess at the beginning of the harvest. What she had done at the winnowing was even more kind than the generosity she had shown at the waving of the first-ripe sheaf. Kindness, that is, to Naomi. Why was this even more kind to Naomi in the eyes of Boaz? Because he discerned not only her motives but how much such an action cost so modest and virtuous a woman. Immediately he appreciates the weighty seed of God in Ruth. There is no chaff here.

In revealing his discernment of Ruth, his words take in her sense of propriety, and he shows that he is fully aware of all that is in her heart. 'Thou hast showed more kindness in the latter end than at the beginning.' In the beginning she had stood by Naomi, she had laboured for Naomi, she had shared her food with Naomi, she had supported Naomi, she had cherished her, she had kept her vow to her, she had proved her worth to her, and she had done so with a sweet submissiveness beautiful to behold. The Moabitess kept her promise when she said, 'Entreat me not to leave thee.' Thou hast shown more kindness, said Boaz, even than that shown at the beginning. How was this? Because of the cost—and Boaz discerned the cost—to Ruth to do such a thing, to go down into the threshingfloor, at night, and lie at the feet of a man, whoever the man. But she denied all her feelings, she did it. She did it for the sake of Naomi and for the cause of the older woman's inheritance.

Such an action violated every natural feeling in Ruth for what was proper and suitable; but she overcame. That is what Boaz recognised instantly. 'Thou hast showed more kindness' than at the first, conspicuous as that was, more kindness in doing a thing like this. He is amazed at the depth of the work of God in her, a work of God in grace, not of herself by the works of the law; a work of the LORD, a work which gave her faith to act by the Spirit, to cast all upon God, though it violated all her natural feelings.

How graciously he sets her heart at rest, telling her that he sees perfectly all that has happened, all that it has cost her, all the chaste integrity of her intention. She presents herself, not for herself, but for the sake of the woman she loved with such devotion, she presents herself, I say, to plead before the lord of the harvest. This was Ruth's faith, a faith instantly vindicated by the man able to discern the true, solid seed from the chaff. He responds, 'Inasmuch as thou followedst not young men, whether poor or rich.' He shows his appreciation of her

116

unselfishness. She had given her whole life to serve Naomi, and she would not be deflected; she had been true to her word, she had ignored her own worldly interests and desires with sublime detachment. She abode with her mother-in-law. She followed not young men, whether poor, such as the virile, youthful harvesters; or rich, such as the mighty man of wealth, Boaz. By these words, he declares his esteem of her worth, whilst assuring her of his knowledge of her integrity.

Boaz continued, 'And now, my daughter, fear not; I will do to thee all that thou requirest: for all the city of my people doth know that thou art a virtuous woman.' This is an answer of grace: 'my daughter'. He owns relationship. Not to Naomi, but to Ruth herself. He would do as she required, for he had discerned the seed of God, the weighty seed, and perceived that it had been well winnowed by the highest of hands, made free from the chaff with its light and vain working. She had proved her worth by the work of faith. And she had found that he knew her past life in a way beyond her imagining: 'I know thy works.' He had found nothing but the solid seed, nothing but worth. His declaration of her virtue was no more than the truth. Whom the LORD loveth, he chasteneth, and scourgeth—or, in the figure of seed, winnoweth—every son whom he receiveth. If ye endure chastening, God dealeth with you as sons. And Boaz dealt with her as a daughter: 'My daughter.' What comfort for Ruth lay in these words.

Boaz now makes a vital disclosure: 'It is true that I am thy near kinsman—*gaal*—howbeit there is a kinsman—*gaal*—nearer than I. Tarry this night, and it shall be in the morning, that if he will perform unto thee the part of a kinsman—*gaal*—well; let him do the kinsman's part: but if he will not do the part of a kinsman—*gaal*—to thee, then will I do the part of a kinsman —*gaal*—to thee, as the LORD liveth: lie down until the morning', Ruth 3:12,13. Boaz reveals a hidden complication. Notice that crucial complication: 'Howbeit there is a kinsman —*gaal*—nearer than I.' Boaz tells Ruth that he will do the part of a kinsman-redeemer unto her, but there is this complication. There is a kinsman-redeemer nearer than him.

Now the law states that Boaz cannot redeem irrespective of the right of this nearer *gaal*. The nearest kinsman has the right, and until that right either be exercised, repudiated, or lawfully challenged, no other kinsman might act the part of a *gaal*. That was the law. And that created the complication. The law was the complication. It was a legal complication. The thing that appeared surprising, however, was the intimate knowledge of Boaz of the precise situation. He was aware of every detail. Ruth came to him in trepidation, but already he knew the situation perfectly. Ruth may have feared that Boaz did not know about the need of Naomi, or of her house, for him to do the part of a *gaal*, but what emerges is that she could add nothing to his knowledge of the situation.

More: not only did Boaz know all that Ruth knew, but he was aware of things of which Ruth had never dreamed. He had already discovered a situation in which there was a *gaal* with prior right, a kinsman-redeemer nearer than himself. This reveals a remarkable circumstance: Ruth did not know of the complication, it was Boaz that disclosed the complication. Ruth was unaware of the situation, she went to him hoping that he would hear her case, but, in fact, he told her things about her case about which she knew nothing. Yet for all this knowledge, he would take no steps until—having taken her life in her hands—she approached him by faith on behalf of Naomi her mother-in-law. Though he was willing to do the part of a kinsman to her, and had the power and resource to perform it, he would not: she must come into a consciousness of need for herself, and come by faith, and approach him as a humble suppliant in consequence.

Thus in the threshingfloor, past midnight, Ruth discovered how wonderfully her faith in Boaz was justified. Not only did he know her case from the beginning, not only did he know to perfection her integrity in the issue: likewise he knew beforehand of difficulties about which she knew nothing. Thus she realised that he was fully conversant with her need, and more than her need. She learned also that had she not acted in faith to make known to him her dependence upon him, had she not made her entreaty for him to act on her behalf, her desires might well have remained frustrated.

Ruth knew nothing of the nearer relative, the first kinsman-redeemer. But was the same true of Naomi? Naomi was a woman who would surely have known of all the circumstances, all the persons involved, all the difficulties. Yet she neither mentioned nor regarded this other, nearer, kinsman-redeemer. Naomi, in her wisdom, was a woman who would have been fully aware of the situation, of all that passed in Bethlehem-judah, as well as everything that was judged in the gate. But she said nothing. She did not inform Ruth of the existence of the nearer kinsman. She had no intention whatsoever of appealing to him for redemption, directly or indirectly, through herself or through Ruth. But why not?

She ignored the nearer, the legally designated, *gaal*. To her, he did not enter into the question. She had no expectation of redemption from that quarter, law or no law. All Naomi's—and all Ruth's—hopes rested in Boaz. They would appeal to Boaz alone. As to Naomi's knowledge of the legally nearer kinsman, she kept this to herself. She would never appeal to such a *gaal*, because she knew that it would end in total loss. The last state would become worse than the first. She knew that she could never resolve the situation, but resolutely she looked to Boaz alone, refusing to look elsewhere. The other kinsman, all the legal complications, she left to Boaz. She could not solve the problems: but he could. And she believed absolutely in his ability and power to overcome all.

Naomi did not enter into the difficulties of the law, or of the legal problem, because she knew from bitter experience that she could resolve nothing. But Boaz could solve everything. Therefore to him and to him alone she directed Ruth by faith. Neither Naomi nor Ruth entered into the complications of the problem of the nearer *gaal*; they neither entered into it, nor meddled with it: they fastened their eyes by faith upon Boaz, and the wisdom of their dependence was fully justified in the issue. Not only would Boaz deal with the nearer kinsman, but he would do so in such a way that the law would be vindicated, the man satisfied, the price paid, and redemption be assured under his own hand, enabling Ruth and Naomi to exclaim with joy unspeakable and full of glory 'I know that my redeemer liveth, and that he shall stand at the latter day upon the earth.'

VII

The Redeemer

BOOK OF RUTH 4:14, *Blessed be the LORD, which hath not left thee this day without a redeemer.*

THE ending of the book of Ruth introduces a tone that is distinct from the preceding chapters. Here it is no longer the bitterness of Naomi, neither do we read of the gleaning of Ruth, nor is it a case of the mother-in-law advising her daughter-in-law concerning the pathway of faith to be followed in the threshingfloor. Naomi and Ruth no longer take the initiative in the closing scenes of the book. This is the chapter of the activity of Boaz.

Naomi and Ruth have cast themselves wholly upon the mercy of Boaz. Their faith has come to rest in his promise concerning their redemption. They had acted in faith, and now they rest in faith. Ruth 3:18, 'Then said she, Sit still, my daughter, until thou know how the matter will fall: for the man will not be in rest, until he have finished the thing this day.' They had gone as far as faith could go, Ruth had ventured into his presence, the matter had been laid before him, she had spoken in his ears, he had heard, he had given his promise. Nothing remained but to trust: to see 'how the matter will fall.' They had been restless, with a kind of spiritual urgency, an activity, a pressing towards the culminating point of the encounter on the threshingfloor. Now the two women are at rest, knowing that their restlessness has been transferred to Boaz, for 'the man will not be in rest, until he have finished the thing this day'. He is the one to move, his activity takes the place of theirs. For their part, they have reached the place where they cease to act even towards him. Theirs is now to 'sit still'.

Not that there was a time when they thought that they could do anything for themselves. From the beginning there was place only for faith with the two women, they had no thought of works: how could they work? they were bankrupt, they had no inheritance, they had nothing to work with, nowhere to labour, they knew from the first that they were wholly cast upon free grace for redemption, a redemption to which they had forfeited all rights. Yet for all that, indeed, because of it, faith was active. They were possessed of a kind of restless disquietude, an urging, a constant seeking at the hand and providence of God by faith, and by faith in Boaz, the man of God's right hand, the seed of Abraham, of the tribe of Judah. To them, he stood in the place of Christ in a figure. And now they had his promise of aid from his own lips. He would act for them. The faith of Naomi and Ruth therefore came to rest, as by faith Boaz rose up on their behalf. They sat still in the belief that—although out of their sight— the promised redeemer would not be in rest until the matter was 'finished this day.'

The last chapter—chapter four—of the book of Ruth records the two conversations of Boaz in the gate of the city, the place where matters were heard and judgment was given. The first of these conversations appears in verses one to eight, and the last in verses nine to twelve. The remainder of the chapter—and the end of the book—tells of the consequences following on from what was determined that day in the gate of the city. Thus it is clear that everything turns on the judgment in the gate. And it is equally evident that the case to be judged was that which had been stated by Boaz during the night which preceded, when Ruth sought her redeemer at the end of the heap of corn in the threshingfloor.

During that previous night Boaz had brought to light a difficulty in the way of redemption unforseen by Ruth as—in answer to the godly counsel of Naomi—she came by faith to the feet of the redeemer. Boaz had answered her, 'And now it is true that I am thy near kinsman: howbeit there is a kinsman nearer than I', Ruth 3:12. This answer revealed that Boaz not only knew of the situation, he perceived a stumblingblock in the way of his acting on their behalf about which they appeared to know nothing. By so much, their redemption was by no means the simple straightforward matter that it seemed to have been at the beginning.

A vast obstacle lay in the way of Boaz' achieving the redemption for which Ruth and Naomi sought. Of this obstacle the two women appeared to be oblivious. But Boaz was far from oblivious, he was fully aware of their case, it was he that brought to light the complex difficulties which stood in the way of his acting as their redeemer. The truth was, Boaz had no clear title to redeem. The right of redemption stood in another, nearer, kinsman, of whom—astonishingly—the women seemed to be unaware. But were they unaware?

Surely it is extraordinary that Naomi never mentioned this other, nearer, redeemer? A redeemer nearer of kin to her husband than Boaz? If Naomi was so well versed in the ways of God, and in the spiritual conditions round about her, if she was so well-known in Bethlehem that after ten years the inhabitants cried, Is this Naomi? how is it that she knew nothing of this nearer kinsman? Why is there no record of her once mentioning this nearest kinsman in connection with redemption? Why indeed, when in the issue the kinsman declared himself willing to redeem? The answer must lie in the realisation that Naomi neither looked for nor desired redemption from such a quarter. To the extent that, setting her eyes steadfastly upon Boaz, Naomi refused to acknowledge so much as the existance of a kinsman nearer to her than him. As to the complex difficulty, Naomi wisely leaves that to Boaz. According to the narrative, no obstacle existed to Ruth and Naomi, save only the discreet task of laying their case at the feet of the only redeemer to whom they will make supplication. It is not that Ruth and Naomi are ignorant or blind, and cannot see the difficulty: it is that they cannot see the difficulty for faith in the ability of the redeemer to overcome every obstacle and bring them in as the redeemed people of his own choice.

Yet however much Boaz may desire the redemption of Naomi and Ruth, he cannot act irrespective of the rights of God written in the law, which he shall surely honour. Neither can Boaz act irrespective of the rights of man according to the legal rule, which he must certainly vindicate. That was the dilemma facing the redeemer. How to secure the redemption of a poor people, circumvent a prior claim upon them, and yet magnify the law and make it honourable. On the one hand if Boaz were to honour the rule of law in the word of God, it seems that he could not fulfil his love in the redemption of his people. On the other hand if Boaz should have mercy and freely redeem his people, it would appear that he could not avoid making void the law. The reconciliation of these mutually exclusive interests brings Boaz into sharp focus throughout the remainder of the book, as the redeemer in his love and wisdom appears in his character as the type or figure of Christ Jesus.

The 'kinsman nearer than I', Ruth 3:12, of whom Boaz had spoken, comes to the fore as the great obstacle in the way of the redemption sought by Naomi and Ruth. This 'other kinsman' becomes the personification of that legal difficulty obstructing the gracious deliverance sought by the two women. Although Boaz was the chosen redeemer of Ruth and Naomi, nevertheless as next of kin the other man had the prior right of redemption in law. This meant in effect that the law itself created an obstacle which appeared to be insurmountable. Boaz could not make void the law, the commandment must not be abrogated, and the legal rule ought never to be made mutable; hence an insoluble problem seemed to be set before the redeemer, a problem personified by 'the kinsman nearer than I'.

It is an extraordinary fact that, as the book reaches its climax with the issue between Boaz and the 'nearer kinsman', the latter remains unnamed. Despite his central importance, the man who stands in Boaz' way is never identified. He remains a mystery. Why is his name not given? After all, other relatively less significant persons are named, such as Orpah, Mahlon, Chilion, even Elimelech. Yet no person—other than Boaz—is more significant to the issue of redemption. The book hinges upon his decision. Then, given such significance, why is he anonymous? If Boaz is typical of Christ, and he is; if the two women, Jew and Gentile, set forth the people of God, and they do; if Elimelech and his sons signify the disobedient Jews, which they were; if all these are named specifically, and they are: why has the nearest kinsman of all, emerging as one of the most representative figures in the book, why, I say, has the nearest kinsman no identity?

Why has the 'nearer kinsman' no name? Because of what he portrays. What he embodies—and must actually personify to give meaning to the figure—is in itself a thing impersonal and objective. Hence the absence of a given name. In the narrative the man is made to typify a pure concept; the concept of the law. He is the very embodiment of the legal difficulties in the way of redemption.

Consider how impersonal the man is made to appear. He has no name; he is a kind of non-person. In the book of Ruth he appears simply as a complex obstacle. He has no personal feeling or involvement; no personality. He neither knows of nor is concerned for the redemption of Naomi and Ruth: he is not in the least troubled about redeeming their land. Does he make any approach? Has he even thought about the destitute women? Have they the least hope of any help from him? Do they even consider going for help to so detached and objective—if not indifferent—a quarter? It is Boaz to whom they go, Boaz to whom the Spirit of God draws attention from the first; it is to Boaz, the very antithesis of this cold and impersonal 'other kinsman'.

However, once the nearer, other kinsman is called to judgment in the gate, it is clear that legal rectitude is what he respects. At the judgment in the gate he is going to do the thing that is right, not the thing that is wrong. Right and wrong, justice and recompense, the legal rule, the knowledge of good and evil, these forensic verities are things which he understands, they are his rule of walk, they govern his conduct, and to such things, having been called to the gate, he will address himself. As to the persons and plight of the poor women, that is a matter of indifference; to all intents and purposes his language is: See thou to that. In terms of pity, or of mercy, their redemption does not so much as enter into his head. As a matter of legal obligation, his own proper rectitude before the law—and nothing else—made the question of their redemption a public issue to him.

To be moved with compassion, to have pity, to volunteer as their redeemer, these things were far from him. He did not once approach the poor women. Pressed in the judgment, required to do what was right by the law, he acted. He would act because it was right. Such a legal principle, however, did not create that disposition of heart which would bring redemption to the bankrupt, just as it did not undertake to seek and to save that which was lost. But Boaz did.

Boaz took ten men of the elders of the city, and, being sat in the gate, said, Sit ye down here. And they sat down. Ten is that round number often used to signify completion in the symbolic use of figures in the scripture. Ten elders would therefore indicate complete wisdom in the gate, so that whatever is resolved must be at once exhaustive and final. This brings forth complete judgment, no loophole will ever come to light. There will be no escape clause. Judgment will be full, it will be complete, nothing will be lacking in final settlement. The judges are to sit, that is, they are to give their entire attention to the matter. They must be at rest, free from preoccupation, they are to be wholly concentrated upon the case brought before them.

What is to be brought before the judgment of the elders in the gate is the question of the lawfulness or unlawfulness of Boaz—who signifies Christ—bringing redemption to the poor of the flock. That is, in view of the prior claim of the commandment and of the legal obligation that stand in the way. How can he redeem lawfully? Can it be done? How can that law whose right of precedent prevents the free exercise of the love of Boaz, be met in such a way that its every commandment and precept may be magnified and made honourable? How can Boaz exercise mercy to the penurious, or give vent to his love for his people so as to redeem them, without abrogating or making void the law which asserts prior claim over them and upon their obligation? Here is a question, the question, to try the elders in the gate, and it is certain that no human wisdom ever was or ever shall be equal to the solution.

It is this legal question that provides all the strength to the case of the Adversary: 'The strength of sin is the law', I Cor. 15:56. Hence it is the inflexible rectitude of the law that we see embodied in the man who—unnamed—sets forth the cold, calculating exactitude of legal righteousness. It is not that the man represents being under the law, or under sin, or that he represents the weakness of the flesh. The man embodies the law: he is the law, and it stands in the way of gracious redemption as a matter of right. The law has prior title to demand redemption by works in the sense that it has first claim over the debtors to outwork their debt, to command 'do this, and live', to require works, and this prior right is inalienable. Moreover, redemption by any other means seems an impossible proposition in view of the inescapable and immutable demands of the commandment: 'The man that doeth them shall live in them'. But it is clear that under the law nothing came forth but disobedience, penury, wrath, death, and condemnation. And shall Naomi and Ruth, after all their bitter experience, look thence for redemption? They have not so learned Christ. But the hypocrite, the bondchild, those that are Abraham's children after the flesh in religion, the Hagarenes, these will look thence, and the reason is, they are not of Christ's sheep. Of them it is written, Ye therefore believe not, because ye are not of my sheep, John 10:26.

The nearer kinsman—the man who embodies the law—had the right over the disinherited, and must claim that right in the nature of law. Boaz seeks a way of redemption which will bring deliverance from the law as such, and, according to the judgment in the gate, so the matter shall be established in perpetuity. If Boaz succeeds, so that the women, impoverished by sin and death, may be freed from that old law, and, indeed, married to another lawfully—Romans 7:1-3—then lawful sentence must be passed at once honouring the precept whilst bringing in everlasting redemption. Thus it shall be fulfilled in those once in bondage 'Ye are become dead to the law by the body of Christ; that ye should be married to another, even to him who is raised from the dead', Romans 7:4. It is precisely this apostolic doctrine which the unfolding issue in the gate of the city sets forth both in type and in shadow.

Notwithstanding—though the doctrine be never so graphically portrayed, or more plainly enacted—none can see these things, much less learn their lessons, save that they are taught of God, as it is written, John 6:45, 'They shall be all taught of God. Every man therefore that hath heard, and hath learned of the Father, cometh unto me'; and none other. The blind legalists, who have neither been taught by the Father, redeemed by the Son, nor led by the Spirit, never learn this lesson. For they will bring the law into the gospel and thereby rob Christ of his bride, his honour, and his glory. We have not so learned Christ, who have been taught of God, and brought into the secret: 'That ye should be married to another', as saith the apostle. 'Now therefore ye are become dead to the law through the body of Christ, that ye should be married to another.' Any form of justification supposed to be wrought on a legal basis, or on a principle of law, such as that of the active obedience theory*, of necessity leaves one alive

*'Justifying Righteousness', Tract for the Times 10, The Publishing Trust. (See Advertising Pages.)

to the law of the old husband, bound to that killing precept, 'so long as he liveth'. This confounds Moses and Christ, law and gospel, faith and works, Sinai and Zion, Sarah and Hagar, the old testament and the new, the flesh and the Spirit, and, indeed, in the event, heaven and hell. This leaves the wretched captives of such a confounded system under the bondage of the law as a rule of life: that is, it leaves them without redemption in any real meaning of the term. Justification must be in terms of free grace alone, first and last, with the old husband dead, and with a lawful deliverance from the law—'I through the law am dead to the law', Galatians 2:19—so that one may be married to another, even to Christ, raised from the dead. This marriage stands in the bond of union as a rule of life, without the works of the law. But how lawfully to be free? That is the question, and Boaz as the figure of Christ, foreshadows the answer.

Then went Boaz up to the gate, and sat him down there: and, behold, the kinsman of whom Boaz spake came by; unto whom he said, Ho, such a one! turn aside, sit down here. And he turned aside, and sat down. Who is this man? Boaz must have known his name: why did he not use it? The fact is, Boaz—through whom the knowledge of this man came to be introduced into the book, Ruth 3:12—never uses the man's name. The careful wording of the Spirit leaves the narrative in such a form that the man—as if de-personalised— is no more than the legal principle which he personifies. He is the legal problem to such a degree that he appears as nothing else in the narrative. And none but the redeemed know how profound and dreadful is the question of the law of God facing the whole of bankrupt and penurious mankind.

Now we know that what things soever the law saith, it saith to them that are under the law: that every mouth may be stopped, and all the world become guilty before God, Romans 3:19. The law demands righteousness, and defines its demands in commandments. Righteousness, if wrought, will earn life. 'The man that doeth them—the commandments—

shall live in them', Galatians 3:12. He shall live, because, if he does the commandments, he shall be counted righteous, or justified, by works. But that no man is justified by the works of the law is evident, for, Cursed is every one that continueth not in all the works of the law to do them. Then, a curse lies heavy upon all mankind, for by the works of the law shall no flesh be justified in his sight, Romans 3:20. That is so, yet man is obliged to keep the righteousness of the law, it is his redemption, 'This do, and thou shalt live'. But what use is such a legal redemption to fallen and bankrupt sinners? As much use as the other kinsman to Naomi and Ruth.

The first kinsman, to whom Naomi was nearer by birth, embodied the law, under which man is born by nature. From nativity the obligations of the law, with both the promised blessing and the threatened curse, devolve upon mankind. The law stands: humanity—given relations with God and man—must come under its dominion. There is no option about law. It demands works, righteously and objectively, according to capacity and accountability, and there is no escaping its inexorable demand: 'This do, and thou shalt live.' If 'do', then by works. Thus redemption from loss must be worked out by hard labour. That is law. In a figure, it is the next of kin. It is, saith the redeemer, 'the kinsman nearer than I'. And how shall man escape such a bondage as this? It is humanly impossible. Only a redeemer possessed of divine wisdom and filled with the love of God could possibly deliver such lawfully bound captives. Naomi and Ruth in their wisdom perceive this, and steadfastly refuse to look elsewhere, or to any other than to Boaz, for their redemption.

Nevertheless, the first kinsman's demands are lawful, and must be honoured, and if the two women will not look at him, Boaz must, and so must the judges in the gate. If Boaz cannot lawfully deliver he must give them up to the inexorable demands of the holy commandments. The nearer kinsman is the principle of the law. He is the legal difficulty in the way of Boaz redeeming poor lost sinners. He is the legal bond of

Paul's 'first husband', he is the dominion over the first man Adam, according to which Adam and his seed must labour for life from the bondage of sin and death. This kinsman is nearer in the flesh and by nature, and his lawful rights shall and must be honoured by the judge. The law enunciates God's commandments to man in the flesh, and it is this same law of commandments that must be kept on pain of death. Man born in the flesh—and man is born in the flesh—appears under the dominion of the law, and that law is the word of God to his condition. This preceded Christ and must be addressed first. Thus this man preceded Boaz: before Boaz can redeem, all this man's legal claims, jurisdictions, rights, and dues must be met fully to the satisfaction of the judges, and to the honour of the most holy law of God. The law cannot be made void, it must not be abrogated; it shall be honoured, and it must be magnified.

This was the dilemma facing Boaz in the gate. How could he redeem, yet magnify the law and make it honourable? To dismiss, to abrogate the law, to set aside or make void the law, would be all the same—in the figure—as if Boaz dismembered or murdered the nearer kinsman in order to circumvent the difficulty. The law must be met, and its demands honoured in full. The law cannot be ignored. And the figure of Boaz and the kinsman in the gate shows—in a simple and early type of the doctrine of Christ—the wonderful principles of the mystery of the gospel through the redemption which is in Christ Jesus.

Then said Boaz to the nearer kinsman, 'Naomi, that is come again out of the country of Moab, selleth a parcel of land, which was our brother Elimelech's: and I thought to advertise thee, saying, Buy it before the inhabitants, and before the elders of my people. If thou wilt redeem it, redeem it: but if thou wilt not redeem it, then tell me, that I may know: for there is none to redeem it beside thee; and I am after thee', Ruth 4:3,4. Boaz' desire to redeem the possession—and hence the livelihood—of the poor, brings him to call the nearer kinsman to judgment in the gate, that the matter of redemption may be raised and settled. The response of the nearer kinsman was never in question: of necessity he consults the rule of law.

What saith the law? 'If thy brother be waxen poor, and hath sold away some of his possession, and if any of his kin come to redeem it, then shall he redeem that which his brother sold', Leviticus 25:25. This means that if an Israelite fell upon hard times—or, as in the case of Elimelech, was stricken by famine—and in consequence sold his land, the inheritance of his fathers, leaving himself without the means of support or the ability to sustain his life, an obligation devolved upon his next of kin. If the next of kin had the money to buy back the field, or if he possessed the ability to pay back what was lost, then the original purchaser who had bought the field was obliged to sell it back: he could not refuse. The field would be repossessed for an inheritance again. The law provided, but did not absolutely command, that the nearest kinsman with sufficient wealth might buy back the field of the poor. That is the law.

Hence, in the first instance, when Boaz proposed the question, 'If thou wilt redeem it, redeem it', he is putting it to this man that he will have to give up a considerable sum of money. Redemption involves the loss of a great deal of substance. Would the man be agreeable to parting with such a sum? That is the first question. What is he going to get back in return? Absolutely nothing. Should he buy back the field, he would buy it back for Naomi, it would bring no profit to him at all, only loss. He would not gain so much as a blade of grass, and, as to the title, it must revert to the heirs. Then, if he redeems, he loses the principal and gains nothing. On the other hand, what happens if he refuses to redeem? What does he lose? He loses face. If he refuses to redeem, he is publicly shamed, before God and man: he has put money before the law, gain before the welfare of his brethren. It would appear therefore, on face value, by putting this question Boaz had miscalculated the willingness of the nearer kinsman to suffer loss. For he would redeem. It seems that Boaz had trapped himself into losing the second right of redemption, by making a public issue in which for shame the nearer kinsman would rather suffer loss than lose face. Had Boaz miscalculated? The truth was, Boaz had only just begun to unfold that profound wisdom by which he was guided in the issue of redemption.

What will the kinsman do? What would the legalist do? What does the law prescribe in such a case? That which is holy, and just, and good. That which is holy: holiness required that he should please God. Therefore the man will part with his money, giving up the substance of his house. The law required that which is just: equity demanded of the man that he sacrifice any amount of his possessions to aid his poor brother, just as, were the position reversed, his brother should in all justice help him in similar straitened circumstances. The law prescribes what is good: it is a good thing to lend to the poor, and require it not again. Indeed, A good man leaveth an inheritance to his children. Once more, A good man showeth favour, and lendeth.

It is written, 'If there be among you a poor man of one of thy brethren within any of thy gates in the land which the LORD thy God giveth thee, thou shalt not harden thine heart, nor shut thine hand from thy poor brother: but thou shalt open thine hand wide unto him, and shalt surely lend him sufficient for his need, in that which he wanteth.' This is the law of the LORD, and to it pertains the rule of holiness, justice and goodness. From these things the legal man will not restrain himself. Boaz knew that, just as he knew that the man would say, I will redeem. There was no miscalculation.

All this Boaz had foreseen. What the nearer kinsman had not foreseen was Boaz' reply. Boaz responded, 'What day thou buyest the field of the hand of Naomi, thou must buy it also of Ruth the Moabitess, the wife of the dead, to raise up the name of the dead upon his inheritance.' By bringing in another precept—and here Boaz' response does bring in another precept—Boaz, who appeared to have been caught on the horns of a dilemma, neatly presents the nearer kinsman with a worse dilemma, and, at that, out of the self same law wherein he trusted for righteousness. Boaz exploits the limitation of the commandment at the very point where it meets that love found only in the gospel. Because Boaz knew the limitation inherent in the law. It was not the gospel, its righteousness did not reach to the righteousness of God. It did not reveal the nature or the character of God. Neither did the love required by the legal precept once approach the love of Christ revealed in the gospel of God. It is precisely the reality of these differences that the nearer kinsman and Boaz personify. One the law, the other the gospel. One Moses, the other Christ. But whereas Boaz fully understood the law—which the legalist did not—the legal kinsman could not begin to understand the first principles of the gospel.

Boaz knew the weakness, the limitation, inherent in the law. Thou shalt love thy neighbour as thyself, yes, but 'Thou must buy it also of the hand of Ruth the Moabitess, the wife of the dead, to raise up the name of the dead upon his inheritance.' Ruth the Moabitess? The Moabitess? That reached to the heart of the legal man with penetrating, icy tones. Yet it was the law: 'If brethren dwell together, and one of them die, and have no child, the wife of the dead shall not marry without unto a stranger: her husband's brother shall go in unto her, and take her to him to wife, and perform the duty of an husband's brother unto her', Deut. 25:5. By connecting the right of redemption—'and he said, I will redeem'—with the duty of raising up seed by marrying the dead brother's wife, Boaz had trapped the legalist in his own rule. For the dead brother had been cursed through disobedience; he was childless because of sin; he was cursed under judgment in Moab; and his widow was this Moabitess, the daughter of the uncircumcised. And shall he go in to such a woman as this? Yes, saith the law.

The decision of the nearer kinsman to redeem—'I will redeem', Ruth 4:4—was taken upon the sole basis that 'Naomi, that is come again out of the country of Moab, selleth a parcel of land, which was our brother Elimelech's.' Legal duty is clear. There could be no question about cost, no selfishness about money. The law was explicit, duty obligatory: 'And he said, I will redeem it.' For holiness, justice, and goodness he will give up all the substance that is required of him. It is not love, or even pity, for Naomi: this nearer kinsman had never approached Naomi; it is duty, it is a matter of law, it is a question of sanctification, of holiness. That is, of his own. He will do it, yes, at any cost he will obey the law. His own sanctification is paramount to him. It is the supreme expression of his self-interest. Therefore, 'I will redeem.' So far, the law.

The law? 'Though I bestow all my goods to feed the poor, and though I give my body to be burned, and have not charity, it profiteth me nothing. Charity suffereth long, and is kind; charity envieth not; charity vaunteth not itself, is not puffed up. Charity doth not behave itself unseemly, seeketh not her own, is not easily provoked, thinketh no evil. Rejoiceth not in iniquity, but rejoiceth in the truth. Beareth all things, believeth all things, hopeth all things, endureth all things. Charity never faileth. And now abideth faith, hope and charity, these three; but the greatest of these is charity.' Charity, Boaz personified, and personified by faith. Legal rectitude, the nearer kinsman embodied, and embodied by the law of works.

The law can effect much, by which a man may mortify his carnal affections, be instructed in his judgment, have his mind corrected in its opinions, and have his memory filled with sound precepts. The law may sanctify a man's whole behaviour, enabling him to say of himself, 'touching the righteousness which is in the law, blameless.' The law may cause a man to reach an extraordinary amount of exterior—and even some degree of interior—righteousness, whereby he may trust in himself that his own righteousness is both sound and sincere, being grateful that he is not as the hypocrites. The law can instruct and inspire a man to make great and numerous sacrifices. It may deliver him from extortion, unrighteousness, adultery, and low living. The law can direct men to consistent fasting—and that twice, not once, a week—regular tithing, continual praying, and repetitive worship. Legal duty and earnest attention to the letter may bring one to speak with the tongues of men and of angels, to prophesy, to understand all mysteries, to possess all knowledge, to have all faith, to remove mountains, to bestow one's goods to feed the poor, and to give one's body to be burned.

Yet withal it is profitless. It is not sufficient righteousness, for 'Except your righteousness shall exceed the righteousness of the scribes and Pharisees, ye shall in no case enter into the kingdom of heaven.' And again, 'They, going about to establish their own righteousness, have not submitted to the righteousness of God.' 'For by the deeds of the law shall no flesh be justified in his sight.' Neither is the love prescribed by the law, 'to love one's neighbour as oneself', sufficient love. 'I know you, that ye have not the love of God in you.' For the love demanded by the law is that which a man must work, and work with futile hard labour, striving at the impossibility of attaining to that height of sanctification without which all is lost.

But, being justified by faith, all that are of faith can say, The love of God is shed abroad in our hearts by the Holy Ghost which is given unto us. Love is of God. This comes through union: not through the law of commandments. Because love is of God, therefore in experience the love of Christ passes knowledge, and in those that are of faith, rooted and grounded in love, consists in being filled with all the fulness of God. That is precisely the difference between Boaz and the nearer kinsman. The law could give every objective direction; and to such things, in the outward man, in the letter, by dint of hard labour, legal rectitude may reach. But it is profitless. It cannot reach to God.

Moreover, at the last, it cannot reach to man. The law may seem to bring in much, in the form of it, but it never did, it never can, and it never will reach to the love of God. It soon appears that the love given by the gospel so far exceeds that demanded by the law, that its divinity abounds over the carnal commandment, as the heavens are high above the earth. The legal man may redeem as a matter of duty, but lose his holiness by associating with a Moabitess he cannot away with. Nevertheless Boaz considered Ruth, and saw what no legalist ever saw: the work of God in the lost sheep. He saw her virtue of love, her steadfastness of faith, her patience of hope, and he knew of a truth that such devotion to Naomi could come from nothing other than the love of God shed abroad in a believing heart.

The nearer kinsman, however, clearly saw a Moabitess, the daughter of the uncircumcised, the widow of a sinful man, and, at that, a man slain under the curse. There could be no question: the legal precision of the judgment, the holiness of the precept, the necessity of divine separation laid upon him were all clear, in view of the nature of this woman. He would pollute himself, he would become defiled, he would render himself unclean, in a word, he would corrupt his own sanctification in Israel, that for which he strove above all—according to the law—by such an unseemly association. Abruptly, he reversed from 'I will redeem', to 'I cannot redeem': caught in a contradiction by the very law in which he trusted. And this shall be the case with all legalists: 'There is one that accuseth you, even Moses, in whom ye trust.'

'And the kinsman said, I cannot redeem it for myself, lest I mar mine own inheritance: redeem thou my right to thyself; for I cannot redeem it', Ruth 4:6. What change is this? In the fourth verse, 'I will redeem'; in the sixth verse, 'I cannot redeem'! What had happened? Boaz' response had happened, recorded in verse five. That response linked together in one the redemption of Naomi's field, and the duty of raising up seed to the dead, that is, taking the Moabitess to wife: 'I cannot redeem.' What an abrupt about-face this created.

But it is not true that he cannot redeem. He can redeem. Otherwise he would not have said at the first, 'I will redeem.' When he said, a moment later, 'I cannot redeem', what he meant was, he would not, and he must not, fulfil the other condition—pressed home through Boaz' response—of raising up seed by a Moabitess. Why not? Boaz knew why not. Because legal holiness, righteousness, and goodness cannot and will not reach to union with the uncircumcised.

Certainly the law required that one raise up seed to one's dead brother, by going in to his widow. Yes, but what the law did not envisage was that such a brother should have gone down to Moab to escape the judgment of God, there to marry the daughter of the uncircumcised, and finally to be over-taken, childless, by the judgment he had sought to elude, dying in the far country under the curse of the law. To take the Moabitess widow of such an one? This was too much for the legalist, stretching the law to a point beyond endurance.

The law is not of grace, and to receive the alien Moabitess required grace, not works. 'And if by grace, then it is no more of works: otherwise grace is no more grace. But if it be of works, then it is no more grace, otherwise work is no more work', Romans 11:6. What Boaz had perceived was an instance where the letter of the law required a thing which the particular circumstances of the case made abhorrent to the holiness of the legal man, and which only a gracious man could fulfil. The letter of the law might appear to require it, but how could the rule of the law condone such a brother as Elimelech, endorsing his disobedience by raising up his seed, and, finally, doing so contrary to the law by requiring one to go in to a Moabitess? 'I cannot redeem it.'

No, but grace can redeem it, because grace is in the spirit of Christ, who was the friend of sinners, who touched the lepers, ate with the publicans, went in to be guest with a man that was a transgressor, allowed himself to be touched by a woman who was a sinner. Grace can redeem the outcast: because grace can say, Rise Peter, kill and eat. Grace can say to Peter before them all, If thou, being a Jew, livest after the manner of the Gentiles, and not as do the Jews, why compellest thou the Gentiles to live as do the Jews? We who are Jews by nature, and not sinners of the Gentiles, knowing that a man is not justified by the works of the law, but by the faith of Jesus Christ, even we have believed in Jesus Christ, that we might be justified by the faith of Christ, and not by the works of the law: for by the works of the law shall no flesh be justified.

Grace will never pass by on the other side. Grace will bear iniquity, take away sins, be made sin, will justify sinners. Grace will have mercy upon whom grace will have mercy, grace will come, with truth, by Jesus Christ. Grace will pronounce, I will, be thou clean; and again, Be of good cheer, thy sins be forgiven thee. Grace will sup with publicans and sinners, lay hands on the diseased, touch the blind, the lame, the deaf, the dumb. Grace will seek and save that which was lost, grace will come not to call the righteous, but sinners to repentance. Grace will kill the fatted calf, grace will bring forth the best robe, grace will put the ring upon the finger, and grace will make merry, saying, This thy brother was dead, and is alive again; and was lost, and is found.

The legal man's desperate hope hangs upon his perfect sanctification for the time being, neither daring to consider the past, nor risking a glance into the future. His justification and his sanctification—like that of the modern Anglicans and Roman Catholics, *vide* ARCIC II*—are all of one, and ever shall be, labouring by works for the approval of an unknown god. Then, in his heart, the legalist knows that his justification is impossible, but from this dreadful truth he hides himself by his assiduous attention to the law for the time

*'The Elect undeceived', Tract for the Times 9, The Publishing Trust. (See Advertising Pages.)

present, by a round of obligations and duties eclipsing all the fearful prospect of the judgment to come. The legalist therefore dares not sully what he supposes to be his holiness. He is fearfully and deeply absorbed with the absolute necessity of attaining to perfect sanctification as the only way in which he can hope to be just before God. Then, he dare not risk pollution by touching the 'unclean thing', which, to him, is synonymous with a Moabitess.

Self-interest, desperation for purity, govern all who would be justified by their own attainments. This is clear from the sevenfold use of personal pronouns in the nearer kinsman's answer to Boaz. He is perfectly absorbed with his own holiness. That is, he is perfectly absorbed with himself. 'I' cannot redeem it for 'myself', lest 'I' mar 'mine' 'own' inheritance: redeem thou 'my' right to thyself; for 'I' cannot redeem it. Perfectly absorbed with himself, how and to whom else shall he pray than 'thus with himself', saying, 'God, I thank thee that I am not as other men are.' Or even as this Moabitess.

To him it was not a question of conscious self-righteousness, or of deliberate self-justification. These things were inherent in, and, indeed, required by the legal system, and hence of all in a legal spirit. Neither was it a question of ill will or contempt for the brother or his Moabitess spouse, though, of necessity, such reflexes were a corollary of being under the law, whether for justification or holiness. It was simply that by being joined to a Moabitess, his own purity would be marred. Redeeming at the expense of legal purity was that to which he could not submit. If that was love, he could not love. It was not that he would not redeem; at whatever cost he would redeem, but taking a Gentile to wife was too much, because he that is joined to a woman is one flesh: they twain shall be one flesh. And if he were joined to his brother's Moabitess as one flesh, it would be at the expense of his own legal rectitude and hard won purity, which he could no more bring himself to do, than he could bring himself to eat with unwashen hands at the table of sinners.

Yet there is a further, deeper motive for this swift reversal from 'I will redeem' to 'I cannot redeem', on the part of the nearer kinsman: 'Lest I mar mine own inheritance', Ruth 4:6. But how would raising up seed to his dead brother mar his inheritance? What does he mean by 'marring his inheritance'? Notice that the legal man does not admit the truth about the limitations of the law, or its failure either to command or generate a love even remotely akin to that which flows so freely by grace. No such admissions of failure or of short-coming will ever escape the lips of the legalist. But the first question every aspirant to holiness should ask himself is this: Is my love of the legal kind? If so, it will fail of grace. But it will not fail either in self-justification, self-centredness or self-righteousness. The direct and truthful answer is therefore avoided: the legalist states what is in effect a diversion, though a truism: 'Lest I mar mine own inheritance.'

But how would raising up seed to his dead brother mar his own inheritance? This is best illustrated from the thirty-eighth chapter of Genesis. This passage records that Judah begat three sons, Er, Onan, and Shelah, Genesis 38:1-5. In the process of time Judah took a wife for Er his firstborn, whose name was Tamar. Now Er, Judah's firstborn, was wicked in the sight of the Lord; and the Lord slew him. And Judah said unto Onan—the second son—go in to thy brother's wife, and marry her, and raise up seed to thy brother. And Onan knew that the seed should not be his; and it came to pass, when he went in unto his brother's wife, that he spilled it on the ground, lest that he should give seed to his brother. And the thing which he did displeased the Lord: wherefore he slew him also, Genesis 38:6-10.

Thus Er, Judah's firstborn, whom the Lord slew because of his wickedness, had no child. He left a childless widow, Tamar. Therefore Er's name—the name and line of inheritance from his father Judah—was cut off out of the land of the living, to be remembered no more forever. Judah, seeing this, lamenting his firstborn and the beginning of his strength, commanded his second son, Onan, to take Tamar the widow to wife, and raise up seed to his dead brother. It is not that Judah took a wife for Onan, his second born, as he did for Er. Had he done that, the seed would have been Onan's. But he gave Tamar, the widow of Er the firstborn, to Onan, for no other purpose than that of raising up seed to his dead brother, the firstborn of his father Judah, through whom ran the direct line of descent and chief portion of the inheritance.

But with the death of Er that direct line of inheritance fell to the next oldest brother. That is, the line of descent now ran through Onan the second born. But if Onan raised up seed to the dead Er through the widow Tamar, his brother would be reckoned to live again in that seed, and thus Onan would lose the portion and lot of the firstborn. By his brother Er's death he had gained the entire inheritance: but by raising up seed to his dead brother he would lose everything that he had gained. That seed, a seed for which he himself would be responsible, would snatch back from him the direct line of descent, the portion of the inheritance of the firstborn, besides all the standing and substance that had come to him as a result of the death of Er.

Yet Onan must go in to Tamar, because he is bound at least to make a show of obeying his father. But he is determined that there should be no conception. Therefore he spilled his seed upon the ground. This was not spite. It was cold calculation. He had no intention of raising up a seed which, though his in fact, would be counted as his firstborn brother's in practice. Why had he no such intention? Because through that seed he should lose everything that had fallen to him—and it was a vast gain—as a result of the strange and unforeseen death of his brother. Gained, that is, until his father, Judah, contrived this scheme. Onan must comply outwardly. But secretly he would make quite sure that nothing came of such a proposal, lest he should impoverish himself, that is, 'lest he should mar his own inheritance.'

This prospect, doubtless, struck gloom and despondency into the heart of Onan. If, at the commandment of his father Judah, he raised up seed to Er, his brother, by Tamar his brother's widow, then Er the firstborn would be counted as living again in that seed. Then Onan would be the instrument of his own impoverishment, raising up seed to his own loss and at his own expense to a brother whose death in wickedness had promised to be such an advantage to himself. Moreover the child would never be regarded as Onan's son; such an issue would be regarded as if it were Er himself. If that happened, all that Onan had gained by the death of Er would be lost at a stroke by his own actions. Everything would revert—not merely to his dead brother—to the child which he had himself begotten, never to be counted as his. That child would by birth attain the status of a firstborn, equal to Er himself—though Onan's own infant—through whom everything briefly held would be for ever forfeit. Inheritance, lineage, line of descent, substance, all would be taken from the second born, and at that by his own begotten infant that would never bear his name.

Therefore he spilt his seed. His child, although born his son and his inferior, technically would become his elder, in standing equal to Er, the firstborn and heir of all. This would not only exclude Onan himself, but should he in turn take a wife, and bear a son, that seed would never be counted in the line of the inheritance. On the other hand, however, any issue born in due course to the child raised up to Er—technically Er's seed but actually Onan's—would cause the hope of Onan, his son, or his son's son, to cease for ever. Meantime Onan would of necessity give up the inheritance and pay respect to the mere infant of his own conceiving, counted as his elder brother. So he spilt the seed. And the thing which he did displeased the LORD: wherefore he slew him also.

Onan refused to raise up seed to his dead brother. Although this was not the reason given by the nearer kinsman for his about-face refusal to redeem the field of Naomi, nevertheless—together with his disdain of Ruth—it was the reason. He had said, 'I cannot redeem it for myself, lest I mar mine own inheritance.' That was not quite true. Had he been strictly truthful he would have said, 'I cannot raise up seed to my dead brother, lest I mar mine own inheritance.' When it was exclusively a matter of redemption, his language was this: 'I will redeem'. But once Boaz pointed out that what time he redeemed the field of Naomi, he must do so also of Ruth the Moabitess, the wife of the dead, to raise up the name of the dead upon his inheritance, then the nearer kinsman reversed his decision, saying 'I cannot redeem'.

What he meant—but for shame did not confess—was precisely the same as Onan: he would not raise up seed to his dead brother, because his love was not equal to the degradation involved. For the love required by the law, and rendered by the legalist, never was and never will be equal to that humiliation suffered by the love of Christ in order to secure the redemption of bankrupt sinners.

Nevertheless Christ did suffer that loss, he did redeem us from the curse of the law, and from its dominion, and in consequence, thanks be unto God, we are not under the law, but under grace. Christ paid the price, that of his own blood, to secure our redemption and our inheritance, not according to the law, but according to his own purpose and grace. He was not obliged to do so: 'I lay down my life of myself.' It was all free grace, that he should give his life for the sheep; and, in giving his life, to redeem them from the law and its curse, satisfying every legal demand and obligation in the body of his flesh through death. 'Wherefore, my brethren, ye also are become dead to the law by the body of Christ; that we should be married to another, even to him who is raised from the dead.'

Boaz paid the price of silver and gold, but, in the antitype, Christ did not redeem us with such corruptible things, but with his own precious blood, as of a lamb without blemish and without spot. Of him we can say, 'Thou wast slain, and hast redeemed us to God by thy blood out of every kindred, and tongue, and people, and nation, and hast made us unto our God kings and priests: and we shall reign on the earth.' This is redemption, and at such a price, redemption that immediately upon payment became effectual, particular and everlasting. When the price was paid the redemption was secured. Because of such a foundation the redeemed are called and set free in their experience to a union of life and fruitfulness, of which the marriage of Boaz and Ruth provided the figure.

Boaz redeemed the mortgaged inheritance of the debtors in Israel for money, and raised up seed to the dead for the life that now is, in this present world. But Christ, at the cost of his own life, redeemed his people from sin, death, the curse, the law, the world, the grave, and the wrath to come, securing for them an everlasting inheritance of eternal glory into which they should enter by a union of life as the bride, the Lamb's wife. This hope of glory, this deliverance from perpetual bankruptcy, this gift of life, this living union, this freedom from the law, by the word of the truth of the gospel, by the sealing of the Spirit, by the work of God, fills the pilgrim people of God with joy unspeakable and full of glory. Sojourners and strangers, separated from the world and worldly religion, they keep the unity of the Spirit in the bond of peace, owning one body, and one Spirit, called in one hope of their calling. As one bride they own one Lord, one faith, one baptism. The love of God is shed abroad in their hearts by the Holy Ghost given unto them, their inward experience testifying of one God and Father of all, who is above all, and through all, and in them all.

Their redemption draweth nigh, and yet their redemption is accomplished. They are redeemed from the old law, the old bondage, and the old yoke. They are not under the law, they are under grace. They do not walk by the legal rule, they walk by the Spirit. They are dead to the law by the body of

Christ, they are married to another, even to him who is raised from the dead. They can say with the apostle, being led by the Spirit into the apostolic foundation of the Christian church by a living ministry, 'But now we are delivered from the law, that being dead wherein we were held; that we should serve in newness of spirit, and not in oldness of the letter.' Their past experience had shown them that the glory must depart from the face of Moses, and this experience had left them in darkness, under condemnation, wrath, and a certain fearful looking for of judgment. But now their Boaz had come forth, and, without their knowledge, redeemed them by his blood, purchasing them for ever, in his everlasting love securing their free redemption, having ransomed them from the power of death and the grave. After that, and only after that, he called them by grace through faith alone.

By a living, interior, marriage union, joined to the Lord in one Spirit—bone of his bone, flesh of his flesh—by the same Spirit they walk in newness of life. That is their rule of walk. It is the rule of a new creation. 'And as many as walk according to this rule, peace be on them, and mercy, and upon the Israel of God.' This peace is what the rule of law never brought, for they know experimentally that the law brought nothing but enmity. Mercy is what the law never gave, but only justice. And a rule of walk is what the law could command but never enable, because all its commandments were only broken continually. How glad, how happy, how blessed are they to be free from the old law, lawfully. 'For I through the law am dead to the law, that I might live unto God', Gal. 2:19.

Once they trembled, supposing redemption of necessity to be by the law of works. And, since, already, they were hopelessly in debt, and quite dead in sin, with every breath and each pulse increasing the vast debt continually, how could they hope for redemption from such a pitiless and legal quarter? They could not, and they did not. Like Naomi and Ruth, taught of God, they look elsewhere. And not in vain, for Christ has appeared on their behalf, and has died for them. Christ has risen for them, and, having purchased them in death, and redeemed them by blood, he proclaims a jubilee to their souls by the Holy Ghost from heaven through the everlasting gospel.

Henceforward they sing a new song, even of praise unto our God, triumphing with one voice, O death, where is thy sting? O grave, where is thy victory? Thanks be unto God, which giveth us the victory through our Lord Jesus Christ. They behold the king in his beauty; they see the land that is very far off. The earnest of their inheritance is their witness to the purchased possession, until that great and marvellous day of the Lord brings redemption nigh, as, raised from the dead at the marriage of the Lamb, they enter into their everlasting heritage.

This is the sure redemption to which all the redeemed of the Lord have been brought, in the fulfilment of that which was signified in the day that Boaz said 'Ye are witnesses this day, that I have bought all that was Elimelech's, and all that was Chilion's and Mahlon's, of the hand of Naomi. Moreover Ruth the Moabitess, the wife of Mahlon, have I purchased to be my wife, to raise up the name of the dead upon his inheritance, that the name of the dead be not cut off from among his brethren, and from the gate of his place: ye are witnesses this day.'

And all the people that were in the gate, and the elders, said, 'We are witnesses. The LORD make the woman that is come into thine house like Rachel and like Leah, which two did build the house of Israel: and do thou worthily in Ephratah, and be famous in Bethlehem: and let thy house be like the house of Pharez, whom Tamar bare unto Judah, of the seed which the LORD shall give thee of this young woman.' So Boaz took Ruth, and she was his wife: and when he went in unto her, the LORD gave her conception, and she bare a son.

Now these are the generations of Pharez: Pharez begat Hezron, and Hezron begat Ram, and Ram begat Amminadab, and Amminadab begat Nashon, and Nashon begat Salmon, and Salmon begat Boaz, and Boaz begat Obed of Ruth, and Obed begat Jesse, and Jesse begat David, of whom, according to the flesh, came Christ. And wherefore did he come? For this cause Christ came, that he might be the mediator of the new testament, 'that by means of death, for the redemption of the transgressions that were under the first testament, they which are called might receive the promise of eternal inheritance.' Now thanks be unto God, which giveth us the victory through our Lord Jesus Christ. Amen.

INDEX

TO OTHER PUBLICATIONS

PSALMS, HYMNS AND SPIRITUAL SONGS

THE PSALMS

OF THE

OLD TESTAMENT

The Psalms of the Old Testament, the result of years of painstaking labour, is an original translation into verse from the Authorised Version, which seeks to present the Psalms in the purest scriptural form possible for singing. Here, for the first time, divine names are rendered as and when they occur in the scripture, the distinction between LORD and Lord has been preserved, and every essential point of doctrine and experience appears with unique perception and fidelity.

The Psalms of the Old Testament is the first part of a trilogy written by John Metcalfe, the second part of which is entitled *Spiritual Songs from the Gospels*, and the last, *The Hymns of the New Testament*. These titles provide unique and accurate metrical versions of passages from the psalms, the gospels and the new testament epistles respectively, and are intended to be used together in the worship of God.

Price £2.50 *(postage extra)*
(hard-case binding, dust-jacket)
ISBN 0 9506366 7 3

SPIRITUAL SONGS

FROM

THE GOSPELS

The *Spiritual Songs from the Gospels*, the result of years of painstaking labour, is an original translation into verse from the Authorised Version, which seeks to present essential parts of the gospels in the purest scriptural form possible for singing. The careful selection from Matthew, Mark, Luke and John, set forth in metrical verse of the highest integrity, enables the singer to sing 'the word of Christ' as if from the scripture itself, 'richly and in all wisdom'; and, above all, in a way that facilitates worship in song of unprecedented fidelity.

The *Spiritual Songs from the Gospels* is the central part of a trilogy written by John Metcalfe, the first part of which is entitled *The Psalms of the Old Testament*, and the last, *The Hymns of the New Testament*. These titles provide unique and accurate metrical versions of passages from the psalms, the gospels and the new testament epistles respectively, and are intended to be used together in the worship of God.

Price £2.50 *(postage extra)*
(hard-case binding, dust-jacket)
ISBN 0 9506366 8 1

THE HYMNS

OF THE

NEW TESTAMENT

The *Hymns of the New Testament*, the result of years of painstaking labour, is an original translation into verse from the Authorised Version, which presents essential parts of the new testament epistles in the purest scriptural form possible for singing. The careful selection from the book of Acts to that of Revelation, set forth in metrical verse of the highest integrity, enables the singer to sing 'the word of Christ' as if from the scripture itself, 'richly and in all wisdom'; and, above all, in a way that facilitates worship in song of unprecedented fidelity.

The *Hymns of the New Testament* is the last part of a trilogy written by John Metcalfe, the first part of which is entitled *The Psalms of the Old Testament*, and the next, *Spiritual Songs from the Gospels*. These titles provide unique and accurate metrical versions of passages from the psalms, the gospels and the new testament epistles respectively, and are intended to be used together in the worship of God.

Price £2.50 *(postage extra)*
(hard-case binding, dust-jacket)
ISBN 0 9506366 9 X

viii

'THE APOSTOLIC FOUNDATION OF THE CHRISTIAN CHURCH' SERIES

FOUNDATIONS UNCOVERED

THE APOSTOLIC FOUNDATION
OF THE
CHRISTIAN CHURCH

Volume I

Foundations Uncovered is a small book of some 37 pages. This is the introduction to the major series: 'The Apostolic Foundation of the Christian Church'.

Rich in truth, the Introduction deals comprehensively with the foundation of the apostolic faith under the descriptive titles: The Word, The Doctrine, The Truth, The Gospel, The Faith, The New Testament, and The Foundation.

The contents of the book reveal: The Fact of the Foundation; The Foundation Uncovered; What the Foundation is not; How the Foundation is Described; and, Being Built upon the Foundation.

'This book comes with the freshness of a new Reformation.'

Price 30p *(postage extra)*
(Laminated cover)
ISBN 0 9506366 5 7

THE BIRTH OF JESUS CHRIST

THE APOSTOLIC FOUNDATION
OF THE
CHRISTIAN CHURCH

Volume II

'The very spirit of adoration and worship rings through the pages of *The Birth of Jesus Christ*.

'The author expresses with great clarity the truths revealed to him in his study of holy scriptures at depth. We are presented here with a totally lofty view of the incarnation.

'John Metcalfe is to be classed amongst the foremost expositors of our age; and his writings have about them that quality of timelessness that makes me sure they will one day take their place among the heritage of truly great Christian works.'

From a review by Rev. David Catterson.

'Uncompromisingly faithful to scripture ... has much to offer which is worth serious consideration ... deeply moving.'

The Expository Times.

Price 95p *(postage extra)*
(Laminated Cover)
ISBN 0 9502515 5 0

THE MESSIAH

THE APOSTOLIC FOUNDATION
OF THE
CHRISTIAN CHURCH

Volume III

The Messiah is a spiritually penetrating and entirely original
exposition of Matthew chapter one to chapter seven from the
trenchant pen of John Metcalfe.

Matthew Chapters One to Seven

GENEALOGY · BIRTH · STAR OF BETHLEHEM
HEROD · FLIGHT TO EGYPT · NAZARETH
JOHN THE BAPTIST · THE BAPTIST'S MINISTRY
JESUS' BAPTISM · ALL RIGHTEOUSNESS FULFILLED
HEAVEN OPENED · THE SPIRIT'S DESCENT
THE TEMPTATION OF JESUS IN THE WILDERNESS
JESUS' MANIFESTATION · THE CALLING · THE TRUE DISCIPLES
THE BEATITUDES · THE SERMON ON THE MOUNT

'Something of the fire of the ancient Hebrew prophet ....
Metcalfe has spiritual and expository potentials of a high order.'

The Life of Faith.

Price £2.45 *(postage extra)*
(425 pages, Laminated Cover)
ISBN 0 9502515 8 5

THE SON OF GOD AND SEED OF DAVID

THE APOSTOLIC FOUNDATION
OF THE
CHRISTIAN CHURCH

Volume IV

The Son of God and Seed of David is the fourth volume in the major work entitled 'The Apostolic Foundation of the Christian Church.'

'The author proceeds to open and allege that Jesus Christ is and ever was *The Son of God*. This greatest of subjects, this most profound of all mysteries, is handled with reverence and with outstanding perception.

'The second part considers *The Seed of David*. What is meant precisely by 'the seed'? And why 'of David'? With prophetic insight the author expounds these essential verities.'

Price £6.95 *(postage extra)*
Hardback 250 pages
Laminated bookjacket
ISBN 1 870039 16 5

CHRIST CRUCIFIED

THE APOSTOLIC FOUNDATION
OF THE
CHRISTIAN CHURCH

Volume V

Christ Crucified the definitive work on the crucifixion, the blood, and the cross of Jesus Christ.

The crucifixion of Jesus Christ witnessed in the Gospels: the gospel according to Matthew; Mark; Luke; John.

The blood of Jesus Christ declared in the Epistles: the shed blood; the blood of purchase; redemption through his blood; the blood of sprinkling; the blood of the covenant.

The doctrine of the cross revealed in the apostolic foundation of the Christian church: the doctrine of the cross; the cross and the body of sin; the cross and the carnal mind; the cross and the law; the offence of the cross; the cross of our Lord Jesus Christ.

Price £6.95 *(postage extra)*
Hardback 300 pages
Laminated bookjacket
ISBN 1 870039 08 4

JUSTIFICATION BY FAITH

THE APOSTOLIC FOUNDATION
OF THE
CHRISTIAN CHURCH

Volume VI

THE HEART OF THE GOSPEL · THE FOUNDATION OF THE CHURCH
THE ISSUE OF ETERNITY
CLEARLY, ORIGINALLY AND POWERFULLY OPENED

The basis · The righteousness of the law
The righteousness of God · The atonement · Justification
Traditional views considered · Righteousness imputed to faith
Faith counted for righteousness · Justification by Faith

'And it came to pass, when Jesus had ended these sayings, the people
were astonished at his doctrine: for he taught them as one having
authority, and not as the scribes.' Matthew 7:28,29.

Price £7.50 (postage extra)
Hardback 375 pages
Laminated bookjacket
ISBN 1870039 11 4

OTHER TITLES

THE RED HEIFER

The Red Heifer was the name given to a sacrifice used by the children of Israel in the Old Testament—as recorded in Numbers 19—in which a heifer was slain and burned. Cedar wood, hyssop and scarlet were cast into the burning, and the ashes were mingled with running water and put in a vessel. It was kept for the children of Israel for a water of separation: it was a purification for sin.

In this unusual book the sacrifice is brought up to date and its relevance to the church today is shown.

Price 75p *(postage extra)*
ISBN 0 9502515 4 2

THE WELLS OF SALVATION

The Wells of Salvation is written from a series of seven powerful addresses preached at Tylers Green. It is a forthright and experimental exposition of Isaiah 12:3, 'Therefore with joy shall ye draw water out of the wells of salvation.'

Price £1.50 *(postage extra)*
(Laminated Cover)
ISBN 0 9502515 6 9

NOAH AND THE FLOOD

Noah and the Flood expounds with vital urgency the man and the message that heralded the end of the old world. The description of the flood itself is vividly realistic. The whole work has an unmistakable ring of authority, and speaks as 'Thus saith the Lord'.

'Mr. Metcalfe makes a skilful use of persuasive eloquence as he challenges the reality of one's profession of faith ... he gives a rousing call to a searching self-examination and evaluation of one's spiritual experience.'

The Monthly Record of the Free Church of Scotland.

Price £1.20 *(postage extra)*
(Laminated Cover)
ISBN 0 9502515 7 7

OF GOD OR MAN?

LIGHT FROM GALATIANS

The Epistle to the Galatians contends for deliverance from the law and from carnal ministry.

The Apostle opens his matter in two ways:

Firstly, Paul vindicates himself and his ministry against those that came not from God above, but from Jerusalem below.

Secondly, he defends the Gospel and evangelical liberty against legal perversions and bondage to the flesh.

Price £1.45 *(postage extra)*
(Laminated Cover)
ISBN 0 9506366 3 0

A QUESTION FOR POPE JOHN PAUL II

As a consequence of his many years spent apart in prayer, lonely vigil, and painstaking study of the scripture, John Metcalfe asks a question and looks for an answer from Pope John Paul II.

Price £1.25. *(postage extra)*
(Laminated Cover)
ISBN 0 9506366 4 9

The Trust announces the publication of a new title

THE BOOK OF RUTH

The Book of Ruth is set against the farming background of old testament Israel at the time of the Judges, the narrative—unfolding the work of God in redemption—being marked by a series of agricultural events.

These events—the famine; the barley harvest; the wheat harvest; the winnowing—possessed a hidden spiritual significance to that community, but, much more, they speak in figure directly to our own times, as the book reveals.

Equally contemporary appear the characters of Ruth, Naomi, Boaz, and the first kinsman, drawn with spiritual perception greatly to the profit of the reader.

Price £4.95 *(postage extra)*
Hardback 200 pages
Laminated bookjacket
ISBN 1 870039 17 3

xxii

'TRACT FOR THE TIMES' SERIES

THE GOSPEL OF GOD

'TRACT FOR THE TIMES' SERIES

The Gospel of God. Beautifully designed, this tract positively describes the gospel under the following headings: The Gospel is of God; The Gospel is Entirely of God; The Gospel is Entire in Itself; The Gospel is Preached; The Gospel Imparts Christ; and, Nothing But the Gospel Imparts Christ.

Price 25p *(postage extra)*
(Laminated Cover)
No. 1 in the Series

THE STRAIT GATE

'TRACT FOR THE TIMES' SERIES

The Strait Gate. Exceptionally well made, this booklet consists of extracts from 'The Messiah', compiled in such a way as to challenge the shallowness of much of today's 'easy-believism', whilst positively pointing to the strait gate.

Price 25p *(postage extra)*
(Laminated Cover)
No. 2 in the Series

ETERNAL SONSHIP
AND TAYLOR BRETHREN

'TRACT FOR THE TIMES' SERIES

Eternal Sonship and Taylor Brethren. This booklet is highly recommended, particularly for those perplexed by James Taylor's teaching against the eternal sonship of Christ.

Price 25p *(postage extra)*
(Laminated Cover)
No. 3 in the Series

MARKS OF THE
NEW TESTAMENT CHURCH
'TRACT FOR THE TIMES' SERIES

Marks of the New Testament Church. This exposition from Acts 2:42 declares what were, and what were not, the abiding marks of the church. The apostles' doctrine, fellowship and ordinances are lucidly explained.

Price 25p *(postage extra)*
(Laminated Cover)
No. 4 in the Series

THE CHARISMATIC DELUSION
'TRACT FOR THE TIMES' SERIES

The Charismatic Delusion. A prophetic message revealing the fundamental error of this movement which has swept away so many in the tide of its popularity. Here the delusion is dispelled.

Price 25p *(postage extra)*
(Laminated Cover)
No. 5 in the Series

PREMILLENNIALISM EXPOSED
'TRACT FOR THE TIMES' SERIES

Premillennialism Exposed. Well received evangelically, particularly through the influence of J.N. Darby, the Schofield bible, and the Plymouth Brethren, Premillennialism has assumed the cloak of orthodoxy. In this tract the cloak is removed, and the unorthodoxy of this system is exposed. A remarkable revelation.

Price 25p *(postage extra)*
(Laminated Cover)
No. 6 in the Series

JUSTIFICATION AND PEACE

'TRACT FOR THE TIMES' SERIES

Justification and Peace. This tract is taken from a message preached in December 1984 at Penang Hill, Malaysia. In this well-known address, peace with God is seen to be based upon nothing save justification by faith. No one should miss this tract.

Price 25p *(postage extra)*
(Laminated Cover)
No. 7 in the Series

FAITH OR PRESUMPTION?

'TRACT FOR THE TIMES' SERIES

Faith or presumption? The eighth tract in this vital series exposes the difference between faith and presumption, showing that faith is not of the law, neither is is apart from the work of God, nor is it of man. The work of God in man that precedes saving faith is opened generally and particularly, and the tract goes on to reveal positively the nature of saving faith. Belief and 'easy-believism' are contrasted, making clear the difference between the two, as the system of presumption—called easy-believism—is clearly shown, and the way of true belief pointed out with lucid clarity.

Price 25p *(postage extra)*
(Laminated Cover)
No. 8 in the Series

THE ELECT UNDECEIVED
'TRACT FOR THE TIMES' SERIES

The Elect undeceived, the ninth Tract for the Times, earnestly contends for 'the faith once delivered to the saints' in a way that is spiritually edifying, positive, and subject to the Lord Jesus Christ according to the scriptures.

The Tract is a response to the pamphlet 'Salvation and the Church' published jointly by the Catholic Truth Society and Church House Publishing, in which the Anglican and Roman Catholic Commissioners agree together about JUSTIFICATION. The pamphlet shows how they have agreed.

Price 25p *(postage extra)*
(Laminated Cover)
No. 9 in the Series

JUSTIFYING RIGHTEOUSNESS
'TRACT FOR THE TIMES' SERIES

Justifying Righteousness. Was it wrought by the law of Moses or by the blood of Christ? Written not in the language of dead theology but that of the living God, here is the vital and experimental doctrine of the new testament. Part of the book 'Justification by Faith', nevertheless this tract has a message in itself essential to those who would know and understand the truth.

Price 25p *(postage extra)*
(Laminated Cover)
No. 10 in the Series

RIGHTEOUSNESS IMPUTED

'TRACT FOR THE TIMES' SERIES

Righteousness Imputed. The truth of the gospel and the fallacy of tradition. Here the gospel trumpet of the jubilee is sounded in no uncertain terms, as on the one hand that truth essential to be believed for salvation is opened from holy scripture, and on the other the errors of Brethrenism are brought to light in a unique and enlightening way. This tract is taken from the book 'Justification by Faith', but in itself it conveys a message of great penetration and clarity.

Price 25p *(postage extra)*
(Laminated Cover)
No. 11 in the Series

THE GREAT DECEPTION

'TRACT FOR THE TIMES' SERIES

The Great Deception. The erosion of Justification by faith. All ministers, every Christian, and each assembly ought not only to possess but to read and reread this prophetic message as the word of the Lord to this generation, set in the context of the age. This tract is part of the book 'Justification by Faith' but contains within itself a message which is at once vital and authoritative.

Price 25p *(postage extra)*
(Laminated Cover)
No. 12 in the Series

A FAMINE IN THE LAND
'TRACT FOR THE TIMES' SERIES

A Famine in the Land. Taken from the Book of Ruth, with telling forcefulness this tract opens conditions exactly parallel to those of our own times. 'Behold, the days come, saith the Lord GOD, that I will send a famine in the land, not a famine of bread, nor a thirst for water, but of hearing the words of the LORD: and they shall wander from sea to sea, and from the north even to the east, they shall run to and fro to seek the word of the LORD, and shall not find it.'

Price 25p *(postage extra)*
(Laminated Cover)
No. 13 in the Series

Newly Published: A Vital Tract

BLOOD AND WATER
'TRACT FOR THE TIMES' SERIES

Blood and Water. Of the four gospels, only John reveals the truth that blood was shed at the cross. When it was shed, Jesus was dead already. With the blood there came forth water. But what do these things mean? With devastating present-day application, this tract tells you what they mean.

Price 25p *(postage extra)*
(Laminated Cover)
No. 14 in the Series

EVANGELICAL TRACTS

EVANGELICAL TRACTS

1. *The Two Prayers of Elijah.* This tract, first printed in 1972, was reprinted in 1982. It shows the spiritual significance of the drought, the cloudburst, and the two prayers of Elijah.
Green card cover, price 10p.

2. *Wounded for our Transgressions.* An evangelical message taken from Isaiah 53. Declaring the salvation of God, this is a tract intended to help those seeking the Saviour and his work.
Gold card cover, price 10p.

3. *The Blood of Sprinkling.* Taken from Hebrews 12:24 this booklet expounds the things to which the people of God are not come, besides those to which they are come. Obvious from the context, this is striking in the exposition. The saving grace of God is clearly preached in this evangelical tract.
Red card cover, price 10p.

4. *The Grace of God that brings Salvation.* An evangelistic address from Titus 2:12—originally preached in South East Asia in 1985—which brings home to the heart the work of God in the salvation of the sinner.
Blue card cover, price 10p.

5. *The Name of Jesus.* First preached to a Chinese congregation in the Far East, this pamphlet declares the reason for and meaning of the name given to the Saviour: 'Thou shalt call his name JESUS: for he shall save his people from their sins.'
Rose card cover, price 10p.

These tracts may be ordered directly from the Trust, or through Bookshops. If money is sent with order, please add letter post allowance.

MINISTRY BY JOHN METCALFE

TAPE MINISTRY BY JOHN METCALFE
FROM ENGLAND AND THE FAR EAST
IS AVAILABLE.

In order to obtain this free recorded ministry, please send your blank cassette (C.90) and the cost of the return postage, including your name and address in block capitals, to the John Metcalfe Publishing Trust, Church Road, Tylers Green, Penn, Bucks, HP10 8LN. Tapelists are available on request.

Owing to the increased demand for the tape ministry, we are unable to supply more than two tapes per order, except in the case of meetings for the hearing of tapes, where a special arrangement can be made.

THE MINISTRY OF THE NEW TESTAMENT

The purpose of this substantial A4 gloss paper magazine is to provide spiritual and experimental ministry with sound doctrine which rightly and prophetically divides the Word of Truth.

Readers of our books will already know the high standards of our publications. They can be confident that these pages will maintain that quality, by giving access to enduring ministry from the past, much of which is derived from sources that are virtually unobtainable today, and publishing a living ministry from the present. Selected articles from the following writers have already been included:

ELI ASHDOWN · JOHN BUNYAN · JOHN BURGON · JOHN CALVIN
DONALD CARGILL · JOHN CENNICK · J.N. DARBY
JOHN FOXE · WILLIAM GADSBY · WILLIAM HUNTINGTON
WILLIAM KELLY · HANSERD KNOLLYS · JAMES LEWIS · MARTIN LUTHER
ROBERT MURRAY MCCHEYNE · JOHN METCALFE
ALEXANDER—SANDY—PEDEN · J.C. PHILPOT · J.B. STONEY
HENRY TANNER · JOHN VINALL · GEORGE WHITEFIELD · J.A. WYLIE

Price £1.75 *(postage included)*
Issued Spring, Summer, Autumn, Winter.

Two new booklets:

1. A Testimony to John Metcalfe's Ministry
   Penang and Singapore 1985 to 1988

2. The Witness of the Congregation Meeting at
   Bethlehem Meeting Hall to John Metcalfe's Ministry 1988

Available free of charge on request from the Publishing Trust.

Book Order Form

Please send to the address below:-

		Price	Quantity
A Question for Pope John Paul II		£1.25	......
Of God or Man?		£1.45	......
Noah and the Flood		£1.20	......
The Red Heifer		£0.75	......
The Wells of Salvation		£1.50	......
The Book of Ruth (Hardback edition)		£4.95	......

Psalms, Hymns & Spiritual Songs (Hardback edition)

		Price	Quantity
The Psalms of the Old Testament		£2.50	......
Spiritual Songs from the Gospels		£2.50	......
The Hymns of the New Testament		£2.50	......

'Apostolic Foundation of the Christian Church' series

		Price	Quantity
Foundations Uncovered	Vol.I	£0.30	......
The Birth of Jesus Christ	Vol.II	£0.95	......
The Messiah	Vol.III	£2.45	......
The Son of God and Seed of David (Hardback edition)	Vol.IV	£6.95	......
Christ Crucified (Hardback edition)	Vol.V	£6.95	......
Justification by Faith (Hardback edition)	Vol.VI	£7.50	......

Tracts

		Price	Quantity
The Two Prayers of Elijah		£0.10	......
Wounded for our Transgressions		£0.10	......
The Blood of Sprinkling		£0.10	......
The Grace of God that Brings Salvation		£0.10	......
The Name of Jesus		£0.10	

'Tract for the Times' series

		Price	Quantity
The Gospel of God	No.1	£0.25	......
The Strait Gate	No.2	£0.25	......
Eternal Sonship and Taylor Brethren	No.3	£0.25	......
Marks of the New Testament Church	No.4	£0.25	......
The Charismatic Delusion	No.5	£0.25	......
Premillennialism Exposed	No.6	£0.25	......
Justification and Peace	No.7	£0.25	......
Faith or presumption?	No.8	£0.25	......
The Elect undeceived	No.9	£0.25	......
Justifying Righteousness	No.10	£0.25	......
Righteousness Imputed	No.11	£0.25	......
The Great Deception	No.12	£0.25	......
A Famine in the Land	No.13	£0.25	......
Blood and Water	No.14	£0.25	......

Name and Address (in block capitals)

. . . .

. . . .

. . . .

If money is sent with order please allow for postage. Please address to:- The
John Metcalfe Publishing Trust, Church Road, Tylers Green, Penn, Bucks, HP10 8LN.

Magazine Order Form

Name and Address (in block capitals)

. . . .

. . . .

. . . .

Please send me .... current copy/copies of The Ministry of the New Testament.

Please send me .... year/s subscription.

I enclose a cheque/postal order for £ ....

(Price: including postage, U.K. £1.75; Overseas £1.90)
(One year's subscription: Including postage, U.K. £7.00; Overseas £7.60)

Cheques should be made payable to The John Metcalfe Publishing Trust, and for overseas subscribers should be in pounds sterling drawn on a London Bank.

10 or more copies to one address will qualify for a 10% discount

Back numbers from Spring 1986 available.

Please send to The John Metcalfe Publishing Trust, Church Road, Tylers Green, Penn, Bucks, HP10 8LN

All Publications of the Trust are subsidised by the Publishers.